Praise for *The Gifts Within*

'Every now and then you meet someone who is just so obviously full of love and wisdom. Tracey McBeath is one of those people. Every time I have listened to her speak or read something she has written; I feel the love and wisdom. In this book I was lucky. I was able to feel it 100 times. Tracey has amazing insight into human nature and the readers of this book are so lucky to be the beneficiaries of her wisdom. Gratitude, Simplicity, Order, Harmony, Beauty & Joy. Tracey covers the six threads of abundant living and a whole lot more. This book can change your life.'—**Professor Peter Brukner OAM**

'*The Gifts Within*, what an inspirational read! I loved Tracey's insights into her life and how she was able to turn it around by changing the way she sees life now. In the world we live in we feel we are being judged or we are judging due to several reasons such as the world of social media that dictate what life should be or look like. Tracey gives you the real-life truths on how we can change the way we hear, see and do life even if we don't agree with other people's actions or words. How we react is so important to make it a positive instead of a negative to live a happier, healthy, and more balanced life. This book gives you the tools and insights to make the changes you need; this is so empowering in changing lifelong habits. Tracey's insights are just what you need at this point in life to live the life you have always wanted with no barriers. Change starts within us, and this book shows anything can be achieved if you believe in you! Thank you, Tracey!'—**Anna Fedele, Spiritual Healer**

‘Tracey has a generosity of spirit that is rare and to be treasured. Through her coaching she has helped people transform their lives, discard the burden of learned behaviours and enter a new phase of wellbeing and self-love. In a time where we are constantly bombarded with the next quick fix and told what we need to make ourselves better people, mothers, lovers, caregivers. This collection of insights makes the invisible visible and shows us that we already have what we need. It is all within us. Tracey shines her light and encourages us to peel back the seal of habitual thought of our own reality—to take a peek into our heart, our thoughts, to sit quietly and see what happens. This collection of insights is truly a gift to be re visited again and again and again. Each time there will be something new to see and you’ll wonder at what appears right in front of you. This is life changing. Get ready!’—**Helena Kastanis, Health Coach**

‘This powerful collection of daily thoughts will help you open your mind and shift your perspective in such a way that you realise how much power you have within yourself to feel in control of your life and truly heal, from the inside out. Tracey provides deep, thought-provoking insights with each entry that gently supports the reader to discover a new way of looking at things. This perspective shift makes every difference in the world. It’s the key to finding true freedom.’—**Michelle Dowker, MSc, ND, Inner Transformation Facilitator**

‘Forever I have lived my life trying to be the person I need to be through others’ expectations. I have sought approval from friends, family and even just acquaintances. I have been the chameleon. I needed to think, they thought, I was the good father, husband, friend. I believed my worth was derived from others' opinions. Tracey's inevitable truths have literally turned my life around. She has guided and inspired me to look within myself, accept the uniqueness of every individual. To know we are not going to agree on everything, but we can still be friends. She also guided me to find something, profound, deep and comforting. My most precious 'core value'. A gift I can give to everyone I know. Understanding how different every human is. Their upbringing and circumstances that made them who they are, just like me, unique, different and very much the same. I will not judge, I will be curious, I will listen. I may not agree but my gift is, I will accept you and your uniqueness. You can trust me; you can be you. It's thanks to Tracey I see my place in the world clearly. I live my life from my own expectations not others. Such a relief, such a wonderful place to be. Tracey was my guide and inspiration to seek. There is no doubt that Tracey's insights found in this book were the trigger for this transformation. Forever grateful.'— **Barry Shipsides, School Teacher (retired)**

'In this carefully curated book Tracey McBeath offers you other windows through which to see your world. She gently guides and encourages you to trust yourself with her words of wisdom. Tracey uses her considerable personal experience and knowledge to offer her readers something that may help when life feels a bit too hard, or you feel stuck in some way. This book is not meant to be read cover to cover but rather opened at random. You will skim past some pages and sit at length with others as the true depth of their meaning resonates with you. I know that the words on these pages will be a source of comfort and inspiration to many who take the opportunity to read them.'—**Katrina Gow, Counsellor and Psychotherapist**

'When we sit for a moment sheltered beneath the canopy of sweet-smelling gums, bare skin to earth, gentle breeze dancing through our hair, dappled sun on our back while charmed by the harmonic tones of a babbling creek, we feel our breath ease. Our thoughts reach with in our soul settles with a sense of calmness and clarity internally. As if we are returning home. Home to where you belong and feel safe yet energized and supported. Lifted and loved. This type of unique experience is what Tracey's book *The Gifts Within* is capable of creating while empowering each and every one of us to be the best us we can be. Be inspired to grow and shine with Tracey's beautiful, crafted inspirations.' —**Dr Carolyn Harris**

'*The Gifts Within* is a beautifully crafted guide to presence and resilience. Each concise insight feels like a personalised coaching session, seamlessly blending emotional wisdom with practical tools. As a Integrative psychotherapist, I appreciate how Tracey's reflections honour the mind–body connection, empowering readers to cultivate greater well-being in just minutes a day. This book is a gift that will certainly connect the reader with their own internal gifts.'—**Natalie West, Clinical Psychotherapist**

‘Tracey McBeath has that incredibly rare gift of communication few others can replicate. Her pearls of wisdom resonate deeply because they come from lived experience. Her shared insights are unique gifts wrapped in humility, sprinkled with a touch of humour, and belong to each and every one of us. I encourage you to walk the road of self-discovery with Tracey, book in hand, and allow her to teach you how to become more resilient; embrace your life; love who you are; and help find your own innate gifts.’—**Belinda Fettke, Health Campaigner**

The Gifts Within

The Gifts Within

100 insights to help you overcome self-doubt and start trusting yourself

Tracey McBeath

First published in 2026 by Green Olive Press on behalf of Tracey McBeath, The Health & Healing Coach
tracey@traceymcbeath.com.au
www.traceymcbeath.com.au

ISBN: 978-0-6451048-7-5

Disclaimer: Although the author and publisher have made every effort to ensure that the information in this book was correct at present time, the author and publisher do not assume in hereby disclaim any liability to any part for any loss, damage, or disruption caused by errors or omissions, whether such errors or omissions result from the negligence, accident, or any other cause.

This book is not intended as a substitute for the medical advice of physicians. The reader should regularly consult a physician in matters relating to his/her health and particularly with respect to any symptoms that may require diagnosis or medical attention.

The views expressed are those of the author alone and should not be taken as expert instruction or commands. The reader is responsible for his or her own actions.

Adherence to all applicable laws and regulations, including international, federal, state, and local governing professional licensing, business practices, advertising, and all other aspects of doing business in Australia, US, Canada, or any other jurisdiction is the sole responsibility of the purchaser or reader.

Any perceived slight of any individual organisation is purely unintentional.

To my darling husband Jim, thank you for seeing in me the things that took me so long to see in myself.

To my five beautiful children Max, Tara, Archie, Paulie and Billy. May you never forget that everything you need is already within you.

Thanks Mum & Dad for all your love and support.

What lies behind us and what lies before us are tiny matters compared to what lies within us.

Ralph Waldo Emerson

Foreword

I first connected with Tracey McBeath via social media and was immediately struck by her strong sense of passion and purpose. As a successful health coach and podcaster, she is bubbling with contagious enthusiasm and love of life, as well as dedication in helping others achieve their goals.

The Gifts Within takes us on a journey of self-discovery and self-love. This beautiful book is an assortment of pep talks helping the reader to connect back to the innate healing capacity that we are born with.

Tracey's many years of experience in coaching others to reach their full potential shines through on these pages. Written with honesty and warmth we are reminded that transformation is a process and that we hold the key.

In each of the 100 insights you will find nuggets of wisdom communicated in an authentic and engaging way. Tracey bursts through the programming and false stories we all hold, gently reminding us that healing, joy, love, resilience, abundance, and peace are all within us: we have just forgotten.

The Gifts Within gives wonderful tips on how we can learn to navigate our emotions, step into our own power, and heal our mind and body. It was a truly enjoyable read filled with inspirational stories mixed with humour and love; and importantly drives home the message that it is up to us to own our choices.

Each page opens up like a gift and it leaves the reader feeling they have just been given a warm hug from their best friend. It will leave you feeling more empowered and far less 'alone' on your journey. I look forward to adding it to my book collection for those days where I just need reminding that I am the creator of my life story.

Lisa Parkinson Roberts PhD. Author, ***A Well Mind***

Introduction

This book was born during the COVID-19 pandemic in 2020 and 2021. It started as a way to share insights of love and hope to my clients, many of whom were suffering immensely. I showed up every day over 100 days to share a truth that had helped me to understand how life worked, because when I understood this, it eased a lot of my suffering. At the 100-day mark, I realised I had inadvertently created a book of insights that others might also find helpful.

In truth though, this book was written over the 10 years preceding the pandemic. At 35 years old, I went through a divorce with 3 very young children. Then at 39 I was told I had fatty liver and prediabetes. It was then that I realised that I was missing some very large puzzle pieces in my understanding of not only what takes to be healthy and vibrant, but the role I was playing in my own life story. Why was it that for 4 years after being told I was getting sick, I still couldn't stop daily drinking or eating processed foods? Why did I continued to rely on others for my own sense of self-worth, and live daily with a deep pit of despair that I was never going to amount to anything?

Through my journey to find answers, I landed on some deep truths that changed my life forever. These truths are now what I share for you within this book. What I am sharing is not what you would typically get from someone in the health space. It's not full of tips, techniques, and more work for you to do. It is in fact, quite the opposite. It's much more about the direction I will be pointing you in.

I will be helping you to connect back to what is innate already within you and showing you how to see beyond what has gotten in the way of your connection to it. You will find many messages repeated. This is because often the most obvious and important realities are often the hardest to see. Impact rarely happens the first time.

If you want to move beyond where you are right now, towards health, healing, joy and love, then come along with me for the next 100 days. When we heal ourselves, we heal the world around us.

I've been through quite a few transformations in my life. But there is no doubt that the hardest of times have been in hindsight, the most precious of gifts. These times have given me the gift to know myself. If you look to where I will point you to, life becomes truly magical.

How to read this book? You can read this book in any way you would like to. Pick it up and read one chapter a day from start to finish or just open it up at any page and see what you see. Each page has something for you if you look and take the time to get quiet. One piece of advice I will give to you that I always give to my clients, is to come with an open mind of curiosity. Don't come looking to confirm what you think you already know. If you do that, you will innocently close yourself off to seeing anything new. Instead, show up as a beginner and see what you see.

Don't rush the process. Learn to sit quietly, still and in reflection. Doing that will create space for insight, and it is this insight that leads to change.

My final piece of wisdom to impart before you head off on your journey through this book is to know no matter where you are sitting right now, there is always more to see. If you're searching for answers just know they are there, you just haven't seen them yet. Perhaps just by looking with fresh eyes at your situation, you will see what you need to see.

May this journey lead you home.

Much love, Tracey xxx

One

What is it that you want? Trust that now is the time to ask the question. Because only dreams give birth to change.

If you don't know what you want, how do you know if what presents itself to you every day is going to take you closer or away from your dreams? How do you know when to say yes or no if you're not clear on what you want?

What do you dream of? Less stress, more energy, deeper connections, more time, less worry about what others think, more energy…

Only dreams give birth to change.

You are the curator of your own contentment and over the coming 100 days I hope to show you how to listen to your heart, which is always speaking to you whether you hear it or not.

Because if not now, then when?

If we wait until a moment presents itself as the 'right time' to start the transformation process, we will be waiting a lifetime. We don't need any magical moment to present itself.

Trust that now is the time.

This journey within will connect you back to your innate wellbeing, your innate confidence, your innate resilience, and show you how to live these truth… and then allow those around you to live their truth.

All you need to be is curious. Curiosity is an amazing gift that allows us to stay open to seeing new things. To question. To be surprised. To grow.

I also know the journey within requires courage. Courage to take a step into the unknown. To look in places you may have never looked before. To not know what you will find. To not know all the answers. To not know how it will turn out.

That used to scare me.

And this fear is what stopped me even trying for so long.

But I know there is a safety net underneath me that will always catch me if I fall. It's there for you too.

Like a net below the trapeze artist.

It is there. Let me show you.

Two

It's not how long you live, but how.

With a little more knowing in your heart about what you want, today I would like you to reflect on this question.

How often in the past have you turned away from all that is unresolved in your heart because you feared questioning?

I did that most of my life.

What if you knew that a year from today you could be living the most creative, joyous, and fulfilling life you could imagine? What would it look like? What changes would you make? How and where would you begin?

Questions are so important, and with a naturally curious mind, we don't need to fear asking them. It's usually not the questions we fear anyway… but the imagined answer we may get.

This is a process that should not be rushed. In today's world, where we want everything now, transformation is a process.

It requires patience and 'getting comfortable with the discomfort' in not knowing the answers right away.

If we can do that, we will hear answers.

Then be open to the changes that the answers will inevitably bring. What's the point in asking and seeking… if we remain closed?

All of this may take some time, but that's okay.

The more patient you are as you continue to look, ask, and live, the more you will see.

Fall in love with the questions.

Three

Wellbeing doesn't come from what you do. It is at the core of your true nature.

When was the last time you felt at peace? Was it yesterday? Last week? Last year? Or maybe, you can't even remember the last time.

Today, I want you to see that you already possess all the inner wisdom, strength, and creativity needed to make your dreams come true. Now, I know this may be hard for you to believe at first, as it was for me when someone showed me this. This can be hard to see because we've also been blessed with an ability to cover it over through the busyness that is our daily lives and busy mind.

And when we can't access our inner resources that come with us at birth, we come to the flawed conclusion that happiness and fulfilment come only from things outside of us.

Understanding what is already within you is the most important piece of the transformation puzzle.

Things outside of us can bring about some sort of

change, but it's rarely the deep lasting change we're looking for. It's often just a blip. When we connect our wellbeing to external forces, we seemingly come to rely on these outside circumstances for our momentum as we speed through life. We are at their mercy.

But we don't have to do that any longer.

We can learn to be the catalyst for our own change.

What can you do to increase your awareness of what is already within you?

This is where you might be tempted to write down a few things and you can if you like—there are no rules—but if you can, try to just sit with what I say. Lean into this 'knowing'. Because I am so sure there will be a small part within you that will have felt this many times during your lifetime.

A big part of seeing your innate brilliance is simply knowing it exists. And the only thing covering it over is the stories of your mind.

Back when I was 35, I was going through a divorce with three children then aged 2, 4, and 6. I remember reading about 6 principles that became my guide to making this inner abundant journey. They were like 6 threads that when woven together created a beautiful tapestry that wrapped me in inner peace, wellbeing, happiness and a sense of security.

These have stayed with me to this day.

This is where we head next.

Four

There were things I said years ago that I no longer agree with today. There were things I did years ago that I don't do anymore. No, I am not two faced, I am simply growing and changing as I should be. As we all should be.

The 6 threads of abundant living: Gratitude, Simplicity, Order, Harmony, Beauty and Joy are your guide on this inner journey.

When I first came across these many years ago, I saw different things then than I do today.

As we evolve, the way we see things evolves as well. That is how it is meant to happen. We are meant to grow and change.

The critical factor is awareness. Spending time increasing your awareness in these areas has the potential to wake you up to the abundance that is already within you.

We have all that we need, and these principles will guide you to see it more clearly.

Firstly, *gratitude*. How often do you do a mental and

spiritual inventory of all that you have? How often do you focus on what's going right, instead of what is going wrong? It's not about positive thoughts, but about seeing at a deeper level the richness that already exists within your life… right now.

When we start to see what is already abundant in our life, we then can give way to *simplicity*. The desire to clear out and realise the essentials of what you need to live well. This helped me cross a lot off my 'to do/ accomplish' list and spend more time revelling in the now. All those things we're told we need to have, need to do, must achieve. Do we really? Or do we need to simply realise all that we already are?

Simplicity then brings with it a sense of *order*, both internally and externally. How often do you wish there was more order in your life? That you had more time in each day?

Doing that mental clear out will naturally create more space to do the things that really matter and stop wasting our precious energy focusing on what doesn't really matter.

Order also helps you to see where your focus truly is. It is in the past or the future, or today? What can we control about the past or the future? We can only control how we live today.

A sense of order brings us *harmony*, which is the inner peace we need to appreciate the *beauty* that surrounds us each day. When was the last time you watched a sunrise or a sunset? And not just watched it, but felt with your whole being the gift that it is to just simply be alive?

Our inner world is always reflected onto our outer world. That means that what goes on within you is what others will see.

When we see the beauty that is all around us, and within us when our mind is at peace, we will naturally open ourselves up to more *joy*.

And who doesn't want to experience more joy? You are allowed to feel joy.

This is the potential richness of the inner journey. Start with your inventory and see where it takes you. You have an amazing journey ahead of you.

Five

'It's impossible,' said Pride
'It's risky,' said Experience
'It's pointless,' said Reason
'Give it a try,' whispered the Heart

The heart knows. Every. Single. Time.

As I was putting youngest son to bed, he asked me, 'Mummy, what does Wisdom mean?'

I said, 'What a brilliant question to ask my darling. Wisdom is when you let your heart guide you through life. It's listening to what's in here [I traced his little heart], and less to what is in here [I touched his head].'

How often do you ignore your heart and instead let Pride, Experience and Reason run the show?

How could they possibly ever know more than your heart knows?

They will try to trick you in to believing that they do. Maybe they have been doing that your whole life.

But they never can know more than what your heart knows. You can count on that.

Six

Wisdom often shows up in life as an inner knowing. You don't know how or why, but you just know. That is wisdom.

How do I know when it's my wisdom or heart speaking? This is a question I get asked often by my clients when I'm teaching them about the wisdom that lives within them.

Let me share a little secret. There's a very easy way to work out if wisdom is speaking.

Wisdom is always kind.

Your habitual brain rarely is. That is where your stories sit of who you think you are and what you're capable of. This is where the same old thoughts come from that say… you can't. You're hopeless. You're not disciplined. You're stupid. You're too old. You're… put in your own. What do you notice your mind say often that you can't do? What labels does it give you?

I know you hear those stories a lot. I do too.

But did you know that's just the brain doing what the brain does, spitting out what has been put in?

Churning out stories born out of what others have said, thought, what you've taken from experience… the thoughts you have believed and listened to your entire life.

Did you know you don't have to pay attention to them? And it doesn't even matter if they're true or not. The question you need to ask yourself is, 'Do you want to go on believing this story your entire life?'

Our feelings are our thinking in action. And when we find ourselves sitting in an unpleasant one, we are not powerless to do nothing. When we notice it, we can step back. See our mind has left the present moment, and that is creating the feeling we're sitting in. It's like we've stepped onto a train that's going nowhere fast, and we might feel out of control. That's because we're not living in anything that is real. We're living in the made-up thoughts of our mind. But just like the train that is out of control, we can step off when we notice. It's this noticing that we get better at. Then we can choose to go through our own doorway to peace. Perhaps it's some breathing. Perhaps it's sitting outside in the sunshine and listening to birds. Maybe it's going for a walk. Have you a collection of things you do that can bring you joy?

Your mind is the window through which you view the world. What we focus on in our mind creates the feeling within our body. If we feel and reconnect with our body, we will get better at knowing when our busy mind is leading us away from our wisdom.

Connecting with our feelings will show us whether we're connecting with the best that is available to us, or whether we're simply staying within the limitations of our habitual mind. For most of us, it's the feelings that we notice first before we notice the specific stories of our mind. So start there. When you feel at peace, you're present and in your wisdom. When you feel not at peace, chances are you've stepped on a thought train.

All you have to do is notice. Then make that incredible connection to your sped up thinking.

Wisdom is the feeling. The feeling of peace. The feeling of knowing.

It's always there, whether we're tuned in to it or not. It's always kind and has unlimited potential.

Our habitual is limited potential. It is your attention to this that keeps you doing the same things repeatedly.

Could you see your thoughts as like a swimming pool? You can choose whether you're in it… or on the edge being an observer.

'*Imagine if we took the time to stand on the edge of our pool, curl up our toes over the edge and just wait and hold that space for ourselves. Watch instead of diving straight in.*' Helena Kastanis

Yes. This is possible for you.

Seven

We see through the lens of our own thoughts.

The answers to everything you seek, the answers to growth, the answers to transformation come when we stop expecting people and things outside of ourselves to look a certain way, and we start addressing our internal environment.

What we reflect to the outside world reflects our inner terrain. When we don't understand this, we think the world outside of us is responsible for all that we feel within.

It is not. The world outside of us is only a suggestion. We are the ones who get to decide how we see what we do.

I spent most of my life expecting my husband and children to make me feel a certain way. When I didn't feel the way I wanted, it was because they hadn't given me what I needed. A huge part of my healing and growth came when I stopped doing this and started to take responsibility for all that I felt inside.

How it works is that we are always living in the

feeling of our thinking.

Feeling is thought in action. I know I've already said this before, and I'm confident I will say it again.

If you have don't have the awareness of what is driving your choices in every day, you will be blown around like a leaf in the wind by other people's opinions, thoughts, and behaviours.

You will blame everyone else for something that is coming from within you.

While it so looks like the outside world has created that feeling you have within you, it is one of life's grandest illusions.

An illusion that many spend their lifetimes chasing.

An illusion that keeps us stuck in trying to manipulate the outside world to change a feeling that's being created within.

An illusion that creates a whole lot of suffering and conflict between people where there just doesn't need to be.

Taking responsibility for my inner world transformed the relationship with everyone in my life… because I released them from being responsible for how I felt.

My inner world was no longer their responsibility. It was mine.

As Rumi said, '*Yesterday I was clever so I wanted to change the world. Today I am wise so I am changing myself.*'

Eight

‘*There are three things that last forever: faith, hope, and love. But the greatest of them all is love.*’—1 Corinthians 13

For some reason, I am stuck with what to write here today. I’ve been sitting at my computer staring out my window waiting for some insight. It usually comes to me when I ask for it.

But today, it’s not coming.

Everything my mind comes up with sounds cliche.

You must love yourself. Be the love. Give love if you want to get love. Love is the answer.

All things every human intellectually knows, yet stuff that isn’t particularly helpful to feel more of it.

I do love Rumi. What does he say?

‘*Your task is not to seek for love, but merely to seek and find all the barriers within yourself that you have built against it.*’

We all have barriers.

We may have been abandoned, we may have had our heart broken, we may have been told we're not lovable, we may have been made a fool of. We may have been treated with disrespect.

All of this may be true.

But none of these need to stop you from feeling the love you deserve.

Love is your essence. Nothing can take it away. It can never be lost, broken, or destroyed.

It only feels so far away from you because of those barriers you've built for your protection and to keep you safe.

But these don't really keep you safe or protected.

They only keep you from life. They keep you from love. They keep you from living a life you deserve to live.

They say we can only ever operate from one of two states. It's either love… or fear.

If you operate from fear most of the time, that's conditioning.

What might change if you started to act from love? If you started to believe that love really is the answer to all that you seek and that this does live within you?

I see love as an action. The daily actions I take towards myself and others.

Do I always feel a loving feeling? No, of course not.

But I know these actions are there waiting for me,

regardless of the feeling I'm sitting in.

Loving thoughts lead to loving feelings. Loving feelings lead to loving actions. Look within yourself for the love and you will find it.

Nine

Everything can be taken from a man but one thing: the last of the human freedoms-to choose one's attitude in any given set of circumstances, to choose one's own way.

Viktor E. Frankl

We have an ability to choose the thoughts that we focus on. And we want to know and understand this deeply because our thoughts become our actions.

If we don't have awareness that our own thinking is driving our behaviour, then we need to create it.

And that doesn't necessarily mean having to go back down your path of childhood to uncover what has happened to create this habitual reaction in you.

All you need to know is, it's coming from you.

When we know this, and we want to move from being reactive (which feels like something is controlling us) to a more considered response that is alignment with where we're wanting to go, then the first thing we need to do is create some space.

Have you ever considered allowing some space toto think about your reaction?

Often, what comes up first is habitual.

I like to call it our 'first responders'. It's the reaction to any situation that we have cultivated by responding to it time and time again. This could look like anything:

It's 5pm
I deserve it
I've had a bad day
I'm bored
He cut me off he's not going to get away with it
I'm always anxious
I will start tomorrow
I've been so good
Just one won't hurt
I don't want to be uncomfortable
Just say yes even though you don't want to
I can't do that

You get the picture.

The ones that come up for you time and time again are the ones that are purely habitual thought.

And if we know we don't have to accept these first responders, we can let them pass and see what other responses might be available to us.

Always get angry when your kids do certain things. Why?

Do you always respond with I can't?

What if you let that go and saw what else might be on offer?

There is literally a buffet of thought available to you. And to access it, all you have to do is stop responding to the first responders.

That's it.

Sounds easy, but like anything that is profoundly true, it isn't easy.

It requires being patient, compassionate and kind with yourself as you put your focus into this.

I promise if you do it, the payoffs are pure magic.

Ten

You are a beautiful work in progress. Find a way to feel joy in the journey. Don't wait until you reach the destination. Because you're already there.

I work with people who are courageously seeking transformation of their body and mind. A big part of the process is to understand that happiness and joy are available to us right now. We don't have to wait until we reach our goal to allow ourselves more joy.

It can be hard to see that this is even possible. Especially if our minds are full of thoughts, stories and beliefs that constantly tell us we're not worthy until we've achieved a certain goal (or get to a certain weight).

The irony is, the more we love who we are, as we are, right here, right now, the more freedom we will find to move forward freely in our journey, unencumbered by unhelpful and limiting beliefs.

The idea that we're not good enough just as we are pushes us around every day.

But it doesn't have to be that way.

The biggest shifts are made in life when we can step back and realise that it's not the thoughts themselves that are the problem. It's our attachment to and belief in those thoughts that are the issue.

You can get to where you want, trust the process and enjoy the journey along the way.

It was once described to me as imagine all your thoughts and beliefs as Band-Aids. They look like they're protecting you, but they're not.

See the illusion that they are and watch them peel off one by one.

Eleven

Just take that first step. Just one. And the next one will be revealed.

We often want to change, but we mostly don't understand the process or are willing to do what is required to change our reality. And I understand this fully, because I lived this too. Remember in the start of the book I said I continued to drink daily and eat chips and ice cream daily for four years after being told I was on the way to type 2 diabetes and already had fatty liver? So I'm not judging. I want to help you to understand why it feels so hard, and what you can do to make it happen for you.

We often want change in a much easier way—simply by wishing for it. We think about it, we want it so much, we read, we listen, we study, we purchase programs… but we ignore the most important part of all, which is taking action.

To change anything in our lives, we must change our daily actions. We must stop doing the things we no longer wish to be doing and start (or continue) doing the actions we know will lead us to our health goals.

And none of that changes unless we make the choice to change what we know we need to change.

I know intellectually you know this. We all do.

But the difficulty comes because we're not built for change. We're built to stay safe, and change is risky. Our minds don't like it, it uses a lot of energy. We will have to step over many thoughts and voices of our mind telling us we don't need to, it's too hard, we don't have to, we don't really want to. We will be tired. We will be pulled back time and time again to what is familiar and comfortable.

But if we don't step over our minds and into action, nothing will change. This day, this week, this month, this year will come and go, and in the blink of an eye, you will be starting down the barrel of the following year.

And nothing will have changed.

How will that make you feel? Do you want to be there?

If the answer is no, then now is the time to step into action.

Let's give it some practise.

What is just one thing you would like (and have in your power) to change? Do you want to eat better? Move more? Watch the sunrise? Sleep better?

Which one is at the top of your list? Work on that *one* first. The funny thing is, the others often flow from just making one choice. A choice to put your health and wellbeing first.

So how do you do this?

Grab a piece of paper, and draw a V. While you're doing that, breathe in acceptance that this is how it is for now. That you are where you are because of every action you have taken to get to this point. But you have within your power and ability to choose differently, which ultimately is what changes your future.

Before every action you make (or don't make), there is a point. A place where you either go one way, or the other. Your conscious awareness of this point is going to gift you with the ability to decide which way you want to go.

Most of the time, we are not aware of this choice point. We not paying attention to the thoughts and feelings preceding our decision. But if we can become aware of this point. we will give ourselves the gift of consciously deciding the action we want to take.

So grab your pen and paper, draw your V, and write the change you want to make at the top. Let's pick a common one: weight loss.

Up the top you write, ***I want to lose weight.***

Then fill in your arrows. Start with your 'away' actions. What are the actions you do that you *know* take you away from this? This is usually easy, we know we do these things. For example: eat processed foods, eat sugar, eat takeaway… things like that. What are the things you do daily that are taking you away from this goal?

Then fill in your 'towards' moves. What are the daily actions you can take that you know will take you towards this goal? Eating real food, having real food in the house, cooking more, eating earlier in the day…

Now, to the hardest part, but the one that will set you free.

Fill in under the V at the bottom the situations, thoughts, and feelings that arise before you make your choice.

What does your mind say? How does it try to sabotage your change efforts? What feelings arise? What fears? What situations? When others pressure you? When you're tired, stressed, upset?

The more you know these, the more awareness you will have that indeed you are sitting at a point of choice. You can either choose to head down the old path that is comfortable and familiar but doesn't lead you to where you deserve to go.

Or you can make a different choice.

A choice that will change your future. One that will feel hard (at first). One that will feel uncomfortable (at first). One that will feel clunky and awkward (at first).

The choice really is yours.

It's all about how aware you are of this truth.

Your daily actions are either taking you towards the health and life that you want… or away.

And what would be the worst thing you could do with this information I've just shared with you?

Nothing! Leave it all up in your head, and don't

take any action from it.

Take the action. Choose action.

Twelve

Focus on your plan, not your mood.

Moods can be tricky to navigate. They are constantly changing, and they're a normal part of the human experience. Everyone has moods. Everyone.

The key is in understanding what we should do when we're in a low one. Often, we want to react, do something, speed up, run away, drink, eat, or whatever when we're in one.

We don't like the feeling, and we've probably created a whole lot of habitual behaviour about what to do when we're in one.

All in an attempt to feel better.

Moods are just like the weather. They are changeable and there's nothing you need to do to change it.

So instead of doing what you've always done from a place of a low mood, why not slow down to see if there is something else available to you?

Stepping back for perspective is literally all you need to do.

Just that one simple thing might be enough to give you clarity.

It's funny how we think everything that goes on in our day creates our mood. The kids get up late, the dishwasher breaks, there is a tissue in the washing. The traffic is terrible, the internet drops out… from a low mood we notice everything that goes wrong.

All stuff that if we were in a better mood, would look totally different to us.

If you notice that your moods go up and down all day on a roller coaster, and you experience something called 'hangries', I encourage you to get off sugar. Sugar is a terrible mood destroyer. It hijacks our brains and bodies.

Many of my clients, including myself, experienced a huge change in our moods once we did quit sugar. So, if this is you, it may be worth giving this a try too.

As well as stepping back and not taking your thinking so seriously from a place of low moods.

There is so much potential for healing when we can put in place both pieces of the puzzle.

Thirteen

The body is a sacred garment. It's your first and last garment; it is what you enter life in and what you depart life with, and it should be treated with honour.
Martha Graham

Today it's about self-love… the most important love there is, from which all love flows.

True self-love is when one understands that the inward journey is the path to freedom.

It is not selfish to reconnect with your true loving self, to free yourself from the burdens of your conditioned beliefs and expectations.

It is full of acceptance of your past and opening up to whatever the future holds.

It's a conscious decision to make the most of the present.

It's standing firm in your own beliefs, while holding space for others to stand in their own beliefs.

It's saying no when you know you should.

It’s taking responsibility for your health.

It’s taking responsibility for your needs.

It’s knowing you’re always doing your best while staying open to having a change of heart… which often comes with reflection.

It is love… without conditions.

It is listening to your inner wisdom that knows when it’s time to slow down.

It’s listening when your body whispers, ‘I need you not to do that anymore.’

Self-love is releasing you from the burdens of your stories.

Fourteen

Gratitude is like wine for the soul. Go on, get drunk.
Rumi

I used to get drunk daily on alcohol. Now I get drunk with gratitude every day. If only that was an overnight transformation.

We hear about the importance of being grateful a lot. And to me, much of it is just words. Lip service in the hope that just saying it will make it a part of our being. That affirmation we think if we say enough, we will eventually believe.

I've done the daily three things I'm grateful for. When I was 35 years old with 3 small young children, I made the decision to leave my first husband. For 2 years I was a single mum, and I credit this time to starting my healing journey. This was when I did my three things I'm grateful for each evening.

But I don't think I really got it. It kind of became a chore. And a process that was very intellectual and mechanical. If I missed a few days, then gratitude seemed like something far away from me. I don't think it made a difference at all in how I lived my days.

What I've seen over my journey since then, is that gratitude is a *way of being*. It's not a practice.

It's a way of seeing the world, showing up in it, and something that comes from deep within your soul.

Your eyes see all you have, not all you don't. You see beauty everywhere because beauty is within your soul. You forgive yourself as easily as you forgive others. You see each day as a blessing, a gift, and a miracle that *you* are here.

So how do you get to a place where you are drunk on gratitude every day?

I wish I knew.

Many will tell you the path (which is just the path they've taken), but the truth is, there isn't one. You must find your own.

What I do know is that you first must *believe* it's possible.

Then you need to give yourself the time to *realign* your environment with your humanness, so you're not stuck in metabolic suffering. This includes your brain. Many people are stuck in a cycle of fast and easy dopamine (from screens, social media, TikTok, shorts, reels, gaming, online shopping, online porn, gambling, sugar, alcohol, drugs… the list goes on). This is where understanding how thoughts drive behaviour will be important.

Then you need to act from gratitude. Gratitude only comes alive when it lives in our actions. This must be first and foremost for yourself.

I don't know when and how long it took me. I just kept the faith and eventually, it was like the fog lifted and I could 'see' it. More correctly, I could feel it. I think I teetered on the edge of it for a few years—some days I saw it, and some days it felt far away.

It wasn't until I learned about the dance of our circadian rhythm that it finally fell into my soul. I truly see the gift of each day with the rising of the sun.

I've had conversations with people before who believe this is such a blinkered and naive view of seeing the world.

Having seen the world through the other lens for most of my life, I can understand their perspective.

There has always been pain and suffering, and there always will be. I can't change that, no matter how much I live from gratitude.

But I know that by living my life from gratitude, I'm much less likely to cause others pain and suffering (particularly the ones I love the most). I'm more likely to be able to be there for them, offer them love and support, and help them heal.

I could never have been that person when I was drinking every day and didn't know who I was. I needed (and thankfully found) a person like me now. One who didn't judge, who didn't tell me how to live my life, who just saw who I was at my heart. One who showed me the way out of my largely self-created misery.

Fifteen

To be yourself in a world that is constantly trying to make you something else is the greatest accomplishment.
Ralph Waldo Emerson

How often do you look in the mirror?

No, not just to do your hair and brush your teeth while your mind is racing at a million miles thinking of all that has to be done.

I mean really look in the mirror.

At you.

No, not at your outer layer.

Right into your deeper soul that is shining bright like a diamond.

I'm guessing not that often.

And I'm also guessing when you do look, all you see is what you don't like.

Is it time you started excavating the real you?

The real you that lives just below the surface underneath the layers of stories, Band-Aids, others' expectations, and social conditioning.

The you that is beautiful, compassionate, loving, capable, resilient, confident.

You simply are all you have been searching for.

There is no greater time than now to accept the invitation to live your life in that truth.

Will it be easy?

No, and it will be at times very uncomfortable for you and for many people around you.

But you were not built for comfort, and it's not your job to keep others comfortable.

Let the journey begin.

It will be the most incredible journey of your life.

Sixteen

Happiness is a choice. You have to choose to be happy.

My kids are such great teachers. They do joy so effortlessly. They experience life in the moment. They show up, they feel, they move on. They don't analyse. They don't over think. And because they don't do that, they can experience the moment, just as it is to them.

So can we, when we see past all those habitual things we've learnt to do as we've grown through life. When we are more present. When we don't judge.

When we just are.

Joy can be found anywhere. We just need to open our eyes and make the choice to see it.

Seventeen

Fear, insecurity, shame, cravings, excitement. These don't come through your body. Energy does. And then your mind slaps a label on it and determines what you experience.

Have you ever thought about what a feeling is? I know it's not the first time I've talked about it in this book, but just in case you've missed it till now, let's discuss it again.

I hadn't thought much about feelings until my healing journey. But they run our lives, don't they. Nearly everything we do is to feel more of what we like and less of what we don't.

Think about holidays and cleaning. Both are done because of a feeling you want to feel, or those you want to avoid feeling if you were not to do those things.

They run our lives and decisions, and it seems we're all in an endless search for how to have more of the good stuff and less of the bad.

But do you know what they are, what they're made of, and how they work?

The way I've been shown is that feelings are fluctuations of energy to which our mind attaches words and stories.

Our left brain interprets, labels, and defines the energy that comes through us. So, when we talk about feelings and emotions, we're experiencing two things: the movement of energy, plus our mind's commentary on that energy. A subjective based story about that energy.

Feelings are the felt part of thought.

When the energy moving through you is low and your mind is thinking about your pet that has passed, your mind calls the energy sadness. When your mind experiences low energy as stagnant and unchanging it might be called depression. When your mind embraces low energy, you might say you're feeling peaceful.

When the energy is faster and you're about to do some public speaking, your mind might call it nervousness. That same energy on a rollercoaster might be exhilarating.

The same one energy is the source of everything.

How you experience it in any given moment is down to the interpretative story your mind happens to tell you. It interprets and labels in an instant, all for it to make sense of life for you and in its attempts to keep you safe.

Fluctuating energy isn't good or bad, comfortable, or uncomfortable… in and of itself.

It is just energy.

The meaning our mind attaches to it is what leads us

to like or dislike what we feel.

And it's what we choose to do with those feelings that then, in turn, dictates our behaviour.

But do we have to do anything about it?

Watch your mind want to dissect this. Let it do its thing, but if you can stay curious, this understanding could free you from being a slave to your feelings and allow you to step into the life of your dreams.

As feelings are what dominate our lives, it makes sense to really understand what they are and where they're coming from.

I just suggested to you they were simply energy that our mind has attached thoughts and stories to. Let's look a little deeper.

When we're talking about feelings and emotions, we're experiencing two things.

The movement of energy

Our mind's commentary on that energy.

Feelings are the 'felt' part of thought.

Your mind interprets and labels in an instant, all because it's doing its job like a champ, which is to make sense of life for you, and keep you safe.

It's neither good nor bad… it's simply energy.

And… They are constantly changing. The root of the word emotion is 'in motion'. But it doesn't always seem like our feelings change quickly does it. In part because the labels become deeply habitual and conditioned.

And because we innocently misunderstand how our experience works; it leads us to mistakenly take these habitual interpretations as truth. They are not 'truth', they're energy with a label.

Feelings are not states that can ever exist outside of thought. While the thought may be hidden from your awareness, and your mind is pointing only to the feelings, they cannot live without an attached thought.

Fear, insecurity, shame, cravings, excitement… don't come through your body. Energy does. And then your mind slaps a label on it and determines what you experience.

That is probably the most important sentence for this insight, so read it a few times.

When you see that the label is not as real or meaningful as it appears, that it's only a mind doing what minds do, feelings don't 'feel' quite the same.

Can you imagine how your life might start to look different if you weren't afraid of any feeling?

A great way to notice when your feelings are starting to run the show is to use what I've created for my clients to use, which I call the traffic light system. This helps you to become more aware when your mind and body are functioning from an old story.

When the green light is on, you're feeling at peace. In the flow (or the 'zone'), the air is clear. Your responses and reactions from this place, you can trust. From this place you can trust yourself to make a conscious and considered choice.

When you start to notice your feelings become a little sharper and more intense—sometimes like they're rising within you ready to explode, the orange light is your warning. Slow down, step back, and only proceed when you feel yourself calming and slowing down. Be cautious about your responses and reactions from this place. Your bandwidth is narrowing your field of vision in response to the stress, and your choices are diminishing.

The red is when you're exploding or reacting. This feels intense, you're angry, super stressed, panicking, and sped up.

Stop. Don't react. Step back and physically remove yourself and your mind from the situation. You are purely reactive in this state and your choices are limited to the ways you've always reacted before. That lizard brain is leading the charge. Your job in this state, once you notice, is to just stop and not react until you feel back on green. Remember your doorway to peace? That will help you reset, and switch to soothe. Remind yourself that whatever you're feeling will pass, and you will regain your bearings and get back into that flow again.

Once you can feel your body relaxing, your mind will naturally become more expansive for you to consider your options. Is this choice in alignment with your values? Is it taking you towards or away from the life you are creating? Is it healing your mind and body or creating more damage?

Each challenging moment has the potential to open your eyes and open your heart.

So, there is the world of feelings. They are a guide as to the quality of your thinking, not your life.

Eighteen

If you don't know what you value, you don't have boundaries. You have reactions, you have people pleasing responses, or walls built out of fear.

I've touched on values a few times already in this book, and now it's time to dive in a little deeper. When I have a new client start with me, one of the first questions I ask is, 'Do you know your core values?'

Not surprisingly, I have never had one client say 'Yes' they know them, and they live by them. Again, this reflects my own healing journey. I didn't know they even existed, let alone them being how I could navigate life. Because if we don't know what we value, as I said above, we can't know if we're living in alignment with who we are. In a society that constantly tells us who to be, what to be, and how much to look outside of yourself, it's no wonder most people don't know what an incredible gift it is to uncover and then start to live by core values.

What are values? You will hear many ways to describe what they are, but over the years of working to uncover my own and now helping thousands of others to land on theirs, I would say they are your way of showing up in the world. They reflect the qualities you want to bring to your actions and are rooted in your core self. They are who you were before the world told you who to be. A quiet and embodied 'knowing'… that beautiful feeling we've talked about before when our actions and our core values align. They are not performing. They are not what you aspire to be, and you can't choose them off a list.

You have to uncover them.

But most people don't even know they even exist as something they can use as an anchor in their lives.

What do you stand for?

Values help us make wiser choices. They are an inner compass guiding you (that quiet voice of wisdom) and giving us a sense of purpose. They provide motivation giving us the strength to do what matters, regardless of what our mind might say, and the subsequent feeling we sit in.

Acting from them is fulfilling—a sense of being true to yourself, living life your way, and behaving like the sort of person you want to be.

We're getting older and time is passing, we have no choice about that. But we do have some say over the direction we take.

We can choose to guide our lives according to other people's desires or our own short-term impulses; or we can choose to guide our lives based on our most deeply held values.

'We are not what has happened to us. We are what

we choose to become.' Carl Yung.

They are yours for the taking.

Maybe your core values are love, kindness, humour, compassion, willingness, honesty, or courage. Whatever they are, they are calling you.

Nineteen

Connection begins with being connected to yourself.

We simply cannot thrive without connection.

A deep and rich connection with oneself, which leads to a rich and deep connection with others.

The problem is that as adults, we can lose sight of our ability to connect with others. Trauma, conditioned beliefs, lack of self-worth, judgments, and fear of being seen… all get in the way of our ability to reconnect to our innate essence and open up our hearts to allow others to love and connect with us as we are.

We risk so much when we don't open ourselves up to connection. We may stay in the illusion of safety, but we miss out on so much love, joy, and intimacy that can only come with open and honest connection.

Like with values, most of us don't realise where the solid ground is.

So often, when we feel lost, adrift in our lives, our first instinct is to look out into the distance to find the nearest shore. But that shore, that solid ground, is within us. The anchor we are searching for is connection, and it is internal.

It is internal. The day you have the profound insight you need around this that changes where you look, is like being hit with a lightning bolt. I remember it within myself, and I have seen it many times with my clients.

It gives you a feeling that you're no longer lost. No longer searching to find 'something' in a place where it never was to begin with. You may not know what you will find, you may not even know what you're looking for.

But you will know that you're finally looking in the right place for that solid ground of trust, truth, connection, and belonging.

Understanding and remembering that we are hardwired for connection is important to start the process of undoing all the internal barriers you have innocently put up to 'protect' yourself and prevent connection. This is where you need to look.

I don't believe you need to know exactly what the incident(s) was, what the fear(s) are, what the barriers are within you. You can search for these for a lifetime, and still not be sure of where they have come from.

I believe it's easier than that. You just have to start to notice when you are sitting back, sitting in fear or showing up as you are. Perhaps you will notice your nervous system automatically responding to the internal fear through a stress response. You are compelled to fight, run, or if these have been running your world for a very long time, you may even freeze.

Either way, your nervous system is responding to the input that is coming from your mind. An inbuilt fear that in this very moment you are in, you are not safe. That if someone was to criticise you, judge you, laugh at you, not support you, think you're silly, your life would be in real danger.

But is this true?

Is your life in danger if others don't accept you as you are?

Not really. Not anymore. Being cast out from the tribe is no longer life-threatening for most of us anyway. But what can be life-threatening is living in this false state of fear when the reality is there is none.

We are reactive from a state of fear. We are acting out of a place of well-drilled habits. We can't access choice or emotional intelligence. We are simply creatures of habit and react accordingly. From this place, we can do and say many things we end up regretting simply because we're not sitting in our wisdom.

What is the answer when you find yourself in this place?

Firstly, you need to start to notice. Notice the reaction of your body, the sped-up thinking, the deep urge to react. What is your body doing? Where are you feeling it in your body?

Once you start to notice this, you can decide to slow down and stop, rather than stay in that red reaction zone. Breathe. Remind yourself you're safe. Stretch. Move outside. Do something that will take you through your doorway of peace. To a calmer place where you know you can then access more choices.

Then question the truth of the story that you're acting from. Reframe it if you can to one that more reflects what is true and reflects your values. Give yourself the space to slowly move towards acting from that truth.

Understand that your nervous system reaction is automatic, just like breathing. It may take some time to stop reacting in the same way, even though you intellectually know you are safe. That's normal, and all a part of the process. Don't fear that or think that it isn't working. You will get better at 'watching' or observing it, then deciding on your conscious action from a more considered place.

The illusion that we can't show up with our hearts wide open and be who we are is what prevents connection.

But without taking this risk, we also risk love.

And love is who we all are. Underneath all the conditioned beliefs that we're not.

Twenty

Insight changes behaviour; intellectual knowledge may not.

This whole book is a collection of 100 insights. I am an insight-based coach. But what does this mean?

I have seen over and over that without insight, intellectual knowledge is meaningless.

Knowledge gives you a fuller perspective on concepts, but it doesn't necessarily affect you personally.

Insight, on the other hand, changes you from the inside out.

When you have a deep and personal insight about something, you see a new truth that tends to affect your behaviour, and it feels like you do not have to 'try' that hard either.

When we start trying to have magical insights, we often don't find them. Usually, that's because we're trying too hard to find them or we're looking for the big lightbulb moments to happen. These are rare.

You might not even realise at all until your behaviour changes or life simply starts to feel different in some relatively subtle or indescribable way.

It sort of looks like 'nothing changes, yet everything is different.'

Creating the space for insight is how insights happen. Giving your intellect a break from having to solve and run your life. Stopping the job of thinking so 'hard' about your 'problem', and when new information comes to you, letting it just wash over you without judgement or evaluation.

Sometimes, we tend to confirm or debunk what we already know without even knowing it. When we do this, our intellect evaluates or judges what we see or hear instead of just allowing it to come in.

You may notice that beautiful part of your brain whose job it is to jump in and analyse it for you, but see if you can resist and just watch it with curiosity.

That witnessing is a game changer.

It allows you to be much more open, curious and inspired with a less active mind, and you will be more likely to hear things that you wouldn't otherwise hear.

This is the start of seeing who you are beyond your habits, thoughts, and emotions. A connection with that place that 'feels like home.'

You no longer need to be anywhere else in life other than where you are. You no longer need to prove your worth to yourself or anyone else.

That place where we become connected to an innerknowing that will be your guide on this short and thrilling rollercoaster ride, we call life.

That inner compass that gifts you with that trust in yourself to handle whatever is thrown your way.

I know some of you have felt glimpses of this place. If you haven't, that's okay.

It's there waiting for you when you're ready to let go of the illusion of control that an overthinking mind gives us.

Twenty One

Going back to the old cupboard is a part of being human.

A few months ago, I changed a few things around in my kitchen. I moved the glasses to a new spot. What I found amazing to watch, is how many times I went to the old cupboard to get a glass. Often it was when I was on 'autopilot', and it wasn't until I opened the old cupboard that it dawned on me that I had moved them.

After about a week or so, I stopped going back to the old cupboard so often, until one day out the blue a few months down the track, I went back there again. What did that mean? Was I undisciplined, broken, lacking or useless? Of course not. I simply had acted on an old brain pathway because my mind was probably somewhere else, and it took me back to the old cupboard.

This is such a great way to highlight just how our brain works when it comes to any habits, and why we should expect to go back to the 'old cupboard' from time to time, no matter what habit we're trying to stop doing.

Depending on what the habit is, we simply love

to judge it or think it means something way more than it does when we end up back in the 'old cupboard'. We love to berate ourselves when we end up back there. We think it means something when we do it, that it says something about our character, about who we are, or maybe that we just don't have it in us to change. But it's never a problem, unless we think it is. And thinking it is a problem only stems from a misunderstanding of thought.

The truth is, it's all just habitual thought that has been ingrained in our brain to help us get things done. Then when we don't want to continue that behaviour anymore, our habitual brain doesn't know that, and it will keep trying to send us there to do the old behaviour. Like any well-worn path, it doesn't become overgrown overnight. It takes time, and an understanding that it is just brain junk that we don't have to pay attention to anymore, is super helpful for anyone wanting to create new pathways (or behaviours). Expecting those pathways to grow overnight is unrealistic.

It's helpful to see that it's not the urge to do our habit that is the problem, it is our reaction to it.

I often get asked, when will I not experience urges to eat carbs or sugar? Well, if I knew that I would probably be a very wealthy woman. That's going to depend on how well worn that path is, and how much thought you have tied to doing that behaviour… which in my experience is usually a whole heap!

But why does it matter if we get the urge to do those behaviours we don't want to do anymore? To me it's just simply an amazing example of how our brain works. We don't have to fear it. We don't have to act on it. We can see it for what it is—a pathway we don't want to walk on anymore and let it go. It might be uncomfortable for a while as our brain continues to send out that message, but again… why does that matter? It's only temporary, it will pass.

It's never the urges that are the problem, but our reactions to it. Even after years of not eating sugar, I still experience the urge to eat it from time to time. But because I know where it's coming from, I am not frightened by it. I certainly don't think it means there is something wrong with me for experiencing them!

Our habitual brain (or lizard brain) is where our habit sits. It can't act, it just sends out messages. But the gift our conscious brain allows us to see, is that we have a choice as to whether we act on it or not. Unless of course we head there without even being aware of it, in which case, we are just on autopilot and not focused on the present moment! Which we all do… and no, we're not defective or broken if we do that. We're a normal human being having a very normal human experience. The less we judge it, the less we think it means something, the quicker we will move on from it.

Change is an internal job that is made so much easier when we understand how it works. When we see that all that is required is awareness and understanding, it all just starts to look a whole lot different and a lot less scary!

What would a world beyond your habits look like for you?

For me it looked like *freedom.*

Twenty Two

You're ok, even when you feel like you're not okay. Humans feel stuff. We don't feel good all the time. The bad days must come. Leave them alone and they will go on their own.
Tara Chamberlain

I was talking with my 19-year-old daughter while I was preparing to give a talk to a group of high school students. I was asked to share ideas on thriving through this final year of school, and beyond. I asked my daughter what she thought I should say. This is what she said.

It's okay to do nothing.

Think of sleep and winding down as a positive thing that you do for you. Not another thing you 'have' to do.

You're okay, even when you feel like you're not okay. Humans feel stuff. We don't feel good all the time. The bad days must come. Leave them alone and they will go on their own. Have a teacher, friend, or your mum to talk to when you need to talk to someone or if you feel sad.

Don't trust your thoughts when you don't feel good. They're lying to you! They trick you into believing you're not good enough! It's not true! Don't listen to them when they're saying those things. Do something fun or go hang out with your friends instead of listening to what they are saying about you. Your thoughts are not you. You don't need to believe them.

Tara was diagnosed with ADHD during her second last year of high school. She told me the things I shared with her around thoughts really helped her to navigate difficult times when her mind wanted to take over. I know she also has shared this wisdom with many of her friends who have also found it helpful. One of her friends said to her, 'You don't walk around all day feeling anxious?' He was surprised to learn that this didn't have to his default setting. 'If only somebody had told me earlier', he said.

Yes. Somebody should have told him earlier. But nobody did because they didn't know either. When we know, we can change things. Until then we don't even know it's an option.

Twenty Three

When the sun disappears, you would never imagine it gone forever, would you?

It's cold here in Melbourne. I personally love the changeable weather that we have here. When I was learning how we all work, the weather was a beautiful teacher.

Maybe it could also be yours.

Just like the weather, our moods, feelings, thoughts, and emotions are constantly in flux as well. Whether we notice it or not, they're changing constantly. That is what is known as our 'psychology'. All the stuff that has come through our minds since we've arrived here.

What I would love you to start to notice is what is underneath all of that. Underneath all the clouds, wind, rain and turmoil. Underneath your psychology.

Which is the sun of your being.

Your inner wellbeing, your inner knowing, that is always there, never changing and can never be destroyed.

Your core values.

We would never question that the sun has gone, even on the darkest of days. It's always there shining brightly behind all that weather.

So is yours, beneath all your psychology.

Seeing who I was from that perspective, rather than what was currently going on in my mind, changed everything. Even the stuff that came up often and had created what I had thought was a permanent part of my personality.

I often had negative thoughts, but I wasn't negative person.

I often had anxious thoughts, but I wasn't an anxious person.

I often had stressful thoughts, but I wasn't a stressful person.

I often had habitual, and repetitive thoughts to do a certain behaviour, but that wasn't who I was either.

Those lightbulb moments changed everything for me.

Because if I wasn't all those things that I 'thought', well then, truly who was I? I still feel a thrill and joy in my heart at that possibility!

I guess I was whoever I wanted to be, whoever I wanted to create at any moment. Who I had been all my life didn't have to define me at all!

All I had to do was to see my beautiful, complete, and healed self already shining in there, regardless of the weather I was experiencing. And whatever the weather, I didn't have to take it too seriously, as I knew it would change, and I knew it wasn't who I was.

I could start to show up to any moment more present to who I truly was and respond to the people and events around me… not to my weather.

What a relief that was for me to see. I wasn't broken, I wasn't lacking, I wasn't incomplete, I wasn't whatever label had been created for me, or I had created for myself. I was me.

That's when it became important for me to work out my values. What my heart wanted. Which was so much easier to do once I saw I wasn't anything my mind told me I was.

How I wanted to treat myself and others around me. My values became my inner compass. My inner light is always there to guide me.

They had been always there my whole life… I had just disconnected from it through the course of my living and the louder my psychology became, the less I could hear my own sunshine.

I didn't have to change my psychology… just like we never have to change the weather. That's not on us. We may just grab an extra jumper or an umbrella, and head out into our life.

All I had to do was to remember who I truly was.

You are the same.

Twenty Four

You are always doing the best you can. Always.

There is always more to see.

When you can understand this, you will be free of your mental restraints.

The level of awareness you have around any situation you experience in life has infinite potential for growth.

When you know this, you can stop blaming and berating yourself for your past behaviours.

They don't need to define you unless you let them.

Thought is the power behind your behaviour. What led you to do what you did, was your thinking. Most of the time we are driven by our habitual thinking. Yet most of us are walking around with zero awareness of this fact.

Awareness of thought is not something that only some people have. Everyone has this capacity to become more aware.

Firstly, we must know this is available.

Secondly, we need to have the courage to look beyond what is habitual and familiar.

When we know this is how we operate ourselves, we then can look up to see that everyone else operates in the same way too.

Their behaviour is coming from their thinking. They too, are only ever doing the best they can, with the thinking that they have.

This doesn't mean there are not consequences for behaviour, and we should accept how others treat us, but it does allow us a few extra levels of compassion and understanding when we know how human beings operate.

The only way we can change our behaviour is to focus on different thought. Usually, it's a tuning out of the habitual, and instead a tuning into the new.

If we don't do that, we can't change, and we will stay locked in that mental prison.

Did you know you had a choice as to which thoughts you could grab hold of?

You don't have a choice as to the thinking that comes in, but you do have a choice as to what you grab hold of.

Seeing yourself as separate from your thoughts, is an easy way to start to create some distance between them and you.

Do you ever say things like, I am stressed, I am not a morning person, I am not confident, I can't do that, I am not a public speaker, I can't cook…?

Well, you are none of those things, you just think you are.

If you're feeling stressed, you just have stressful thinking. You're not stressed, you are calm underneath your turbulent thoughts.

You are confident, you just think you're not.

You can cook, you just have never learnt properly.

Can you see?

You can always change the way you look at things. It truly is our greatest freedom.

Twenty Five

With curiosity as your companion, you can change anyone's mind. But only if you can first open your own.

We all can only ever see the world through the lens of our own unique human experience.

Gaining insight into this reality as human beings has been life changing for me, and now also within my coaching work. Often my clients and colleagues feel a sense of despair and frustration because their family, friends or colleagues don't agree or support them as they try to improve their health through lifestyle and nutrition.

Perhaps sharing my understanding of what is going on here might help to ease the angst and indeed create the environment for deeper more impactful connections.

If you've ever travelled to non-western countries, you will be aware of the vast differences among cultures.

Well, what's interesting is that the differences between individuals is every bit as vast as these cultural differences are.

We wouldn't expect people of different cultures to see or do things as we would (well maybe some people do, but overall, we accept their difference with ease) yet understanding that an individual is made up entirely of their own very personal and unique thought system means the same expectation should be applied across the board of humans on earth.

It's not a matter of tolerating differences in others, but it's about understanding that it literally cannot be any other way. It is impossible given the way human beings work to see things precisely alike as this, is totally dependent on input—our parents, our background, experiences, interpretations, memory, selective perception, circumstances, our mood level and more.

There are no exceptions to this rule.

They say 'variety is the spice of life' but most people really don't believe or understand that truth.

But now you will.

The trick in believing this is not to force yourself to think this way, but to see that from a psychological perspective, differences between people and the ways they see life make complete sense.

So, with this understanding in mind, we can then see that it is futile to try to change others.

And nor do we have to.

Problems within any relationship usually come about because we either think others around us should think in the same way as we do; or we think others should see the world in the way that we do because what we see, is the true reality.

Basically, that means we think the way we see it is right and the only way to see things, and everyone else is wrong.

Both misunderstandings cause conflict, resentment and confusion, which is never the breeding ground for connection and growth.

This understanding makes it possible to be freed from a false idea that we need others to see things as we do for our own validation and instead brings the joy back into our differences.

It also logically makes sense too, that we don't need to take personally what others do or say.

People will spend a whole lifetime proving to themselves that their own personal version of life is valid, realistic, and accurate.

That is the self-validating aspect to thought systems which trips us up all the time.

We try to change someone's mind by arguing with them or pushing our own point on them, but the fact is that all this does is push the other person even deeper into their own thought system. Watch a carnivore argue with a vegan and you will see this all in action.

So, within your own family or workplace can you see that it's impossible for you to all see things in the same way?

So why then, do we feel that we must create that place where everyone does see things the same way?

It may have worked to keep us a part of the tribe for our survival as we evolved, however in the modern world it keeps us from seeing and accepting others as they are and keeps us all stuck in our own limiting beliefs.

It's such a perfectly innocent process and understanding it will truly bring us closer to those we know and love.

It helps us to understand others, and it also makes ourselves much more interesting and accessible.

Truly understanding that our ideas about life come from our thought systems and do not necessarily represent reality, draws other people to us.

All of us have a vested interest in validating our own beliefs, and we don't like to have our own beliefs threatened or tampered with.

So, with this in mind when you approach someone, not in an attempt to change their beliefs but with a genuine interest in and respect for their view of life, defences drop and hearts open.

People who deeply accept the fact of separate realities, often have more fulfilling relationships, including with people they thought they could not possibly like.

What used to be a sense of frustration and anger when someone had a view different to yours can be replaced with curiosity. And the more curiosity and understanding you have about how we work when it comes to thought systems, the more likely you will be able to have an impact on others around you.

Because you're freeing them to make their own

decisions, without needing to compromise your own.

Understanding how this works opens channels for deeper connections.

When we know what our thought system is set to do—to validate our own and dig down even deeper in the face of difference—we don't have to be tricked by it and follow that line of thinking.

Because when we do, we're up in our head waiting for a chance to spring forth our own argument.

Instead of truly listening to the viewpoint of others.

Listening is one of the most underrated skills human beings possess.

We're so busy justifying our own thought system in our heads and spewing it out on to others we rarely sit and listen to someone without anything in our own mind.

Have you ever been with someone who truly listened to you?

You will know it because you will feel it.

When you're with someone who is interested in you and what you have to say without needing to change your mind, you set the foundations for a deep connection.

This is the breeding ground of growth.

What I believe is what I believe, but I know there is always more to see.

I also know that people are free to believe as they want and to live their lives as they want too. I don't need to change anyone to have my views validated.

And if I really want other people to be able to live from a freer mind not dictated and limited by their own individual thought systems, the best thing I can do is to bring to the table the opportunity for connection.

Could you see the benefits of understanding this in your life?

Can you see how you're really okay to have your beliefs about what to eat and what to value… but so is everybody else?

Would this change the relationships within your house or work if you accepted your partner or colleague believing differently to you, but still valuing their contribution and connection?

Twenty Six

You are not a problem to be solved.

Your mind may instantly disagree with this. But what if I'm right?

What if you already have all you need to reconnect back to your mental wellbeing? You know, that place inside of you that is there underneath all your psychology, and when you're in there, feels like peace.

Einstein once famously said, 'you can't solve a problem at the same level of thinking that created the problem.'

Yet… that's what our minds want to jump to do. See all the things we do 'wrong' in our lives and jump in to try and solve them with the intellect.

That looks like constant reading, learning, anxiously trying to find that magic pill that will give you relief from your habit. All the things that create a sped up and anxious feeling—because we feel lost—which leads to us making poorer choices simply because we don't have the consciousness to access the choices available.

And for most then, we simply don't do the work. We do all we can to avoid it. Innocently of course. We don't want to feel any more pain than we've been feeling for as long as we can remember.

The only problem with that is it gets you nowhere, and your mind just goes deeper into the illusion that must solve 'you'.

This week, I want you to just stop if you can trying to solve your problems. Park what you think is your problem 'over there'. Don't worry, you can always go back to it in a week and continue the same path to solve yourself if you need to.

But I want you to see if you can see something new when you're not actively 'trying' to solve your thought created problem.

I realise this may seem a little scary—of course anything we do outside of that part of the brain that wants to constantly drive you, will feel that way. It may say 'but without my constant working on it, I will give up'. Or even if you think that 'there's no way you can do that because without your constant focus on your problem, you won't have any control.'

These tricks are all designed to stop you increasing your conscious awareness, which then may lead to you doing that risky thing called change.

Did you ever squish your nose up onto the window as a kid to try and see more inside?

This is kind of like what humans do when they're trying to solve their own problem. Only thing is that when we do that, we're not creating any space for insight… and it's insight that Einstein knew would change the level of thinking. It takes up that elevator of awareness so you can see more… so you can access all the choices you really do have.

When we step back from what we're trying to solve, we allow space for us to tap into the universal internet we're all automatically connected with. That place where we find a better feeling, more peace, and lots of insights we can follow.

Sure, intellectual knowledge is important. But it's not where the answers are for what you're seeking.

They're already within you. You already know it all. You just can't hear it because of your sped up busy mind, hell bent on solving you for you.

I can't tell you how many times I've talked to people who know this. They even tell others to do this. They've got more knowledge than me on virtually every subject related to health.

And yet.

They still can't stop doing their habits. They still feel like they're not directing their own life. They feel like a failure and they're full of shame.

But they haven't done the inner work. The inner work of stepping back from that part of the mind that wants to solve it all. They haven't stepped back from the window to get a good view of the entire house.

There's a story that goes, if you lost your keys inside the house, and yet you only searched for them outside, you will never find them no matter how hard you look.

The same for us all. The answers you seek are already within you. You must stop searching outside of yourself to find that which can only be accessed within.

Can you park your 'trying' and 'learning' and 'searching' to solve yourself for a little bit?

You may just see some things that will shift you in the right direction.

You may even find life becomes a little more (or a lot more) peaceful, you're not as tired from all that brain work, and you start to notice a whole lot more good stuff that's around you. All of which will lead to you seeing what's already available to you.

Wouldn't that be worth pushing through that discomfort just for a moment, taking your hands off the wheel?

We are built to fly. You just need to see you already have wings.

Twenty Seven

When did you feel the most attractive?

Today I want you to reflect on when you have felt attractive. I will share with you when I did. But I wasn't looking 'attractive' by societies standards.

Popular culture loves to talk about attractiveness superficially.

But I want you to be able to see your beauty way deeper than that.

And to spend time cultivating this truth in your everyday moments.

I remember when I was in hospital having just given birth to my fifth child, I was cuddling my boy on my chest at 3am when a midwife came in the room. I remember it so clearly, she said, 'Oh you look so beautiful, give me your phone so I can take a photo.'

I remember saying, 'Oh my God, I so don't. Please don't take my photo!'

I'm so grateful she ignored me and took it. As I know

now, I really did look beautiful then, because I was present to the sound of my new little boy, his beautiful smell, his tiny fingers, his peaceful breath on my chest. I was fully in the moment, with him. That is what makes us beautiful.

What have I seen when I've reflected on the times in my life when I've felt the most beautiful?

The situations were all different, but there was one common denominator: love.

Love was what transformed me, not the outer trappings.

Love for my children, love for my husband, love for my work. Love for myself.

I believe that this is perhaps one of the most important beauty lessons any of us can learn.

Love has the power to transcend our physical limitations.

Let us continuously search for the wonder of it all.

If we do, we can't help but notice the love bubbling up from within.

When wonder and love become indispensable to you, you will radiate an incredible energy that will draw people to you.

Twenty Eight

Science has shown that people who are physically active are happier!

I couldn't imagine not incorporating some sort of movement into most of my days. It's become so much a part of my psyche that I have very little thinking about it, other than when in my day I can fit some in.

And there's some pretty good reasons why you should look to make it effortless too, essentially just get out of your own way and build some daily movement into your life.

The joy of movement can be found in any exercise: walking, running, swimming, dancing, biking, playing sport, lifting weights, doing yoga. People who are regularly active have a greater sense of purpose, and they experience more gratitude, love and hope.

They feel more connected to their communities and are less likely to suffer from depression, according to Kelly McGonigal.

Most often we hear the reasons behind this as being

the result of an endorphin rush, but according to Kelly, these are far too simplistic.

Our entire biology was engineered to reward us for moving.

Physical activity influences many brain chemicals, including those that give you energy, alleviate worry, and help you bond with others.

It reduces inflammation in the brain, which over time can protect against depression, anxiety, and loneliness.

Regular movement remodels the physical structure of your brain, to make you more receptive to joy and social connection.

The mind-altering effects of exercise are even embedded in your musculature.

During physical activity, muscles secrete hormones into your blood stream that make your brain more resilient to stress. This is what scientists call 'hope molecules'.

At a most fundamental level, rewarding movement is how your brain and body encourage you to participate in life.

If you are willing to move, your muscles will give you hope.

Your brain will orchestrate pleasure!

And your entire physiology will adjust to help you find the energy, purpose, and courage you need to keep going.

Pretty much what we all need right now, right?

Twenty Nine

Our habits are rarely about pleasure. They're far more likely to be about avoidance. Something we do to avoid discomfort. The urge feels uncomfortable, and we act on our habit to feel a release from that urge.

What if your habit isn't personal?

Hear me out on this one, because your mind makes everything personal remember? So, this may take a little bit of time for you to step past your own thinking to even want to consider this idea.

Seeing my habits as not who I am, was a huge part of my healing, and it transformed the relationship I had with them.

And it's probably where I break ranks with 'traditional' views of addiction treatments that puts you in the equation in a more meaningful way. They see something is 'lacking' or wrong with you in some way, and that's why you have your habit. Your habit is who you are, and you must own it. Well, in my experience, that just keeps you living in fear of it. Let me explain further.

What if it's not like that at all, and your habit has nothing to do with you? What if your urges are providing you with helpful information? What if your habit has nothing to do with your character or circumstances?

Our habits are rarely about pleasure. They're far more likely to be about avoidance. Something we do to avoid discomfort. The urge feels uncomfortable, and we act on our habit to feel a release from that urge.

They are thought energy that feels compelling but are really quite impersonal.

We live in a steady stream of thought 24/7. Hopefully you're becoming a whole lot more aware of that. These thoughts aren't 'you'—they are simply life flowing through you. And we know it's all flowing, coming and going.

In my innocence, I unknowingly set my habit in motion with my thinking ABOUT my thinking, and with what I believed about my urges. Which I thought were dangerous, personal, unbearable, permanent… which meant I would naturally follow them. I didn't see choice in those moments… until I started to understand thought… and how it really didn't have anything to do with me.

No habit could ever be an indicator of your worth as a human being. Please read that a few times. Your worth is not tied to your habit.

Seeing that, it became so much easier for me to dismiss them and let them pass.

The feeling (energy) you experience when you have an urge to do your habit is a helpful warning sign. That dashboard on your car engine telling you something needs your attention.

It's telling you to slow down and become suspicious of the way you are using your power of thought. Because we are only ever living in a feeling of our own thoughts—and urges are just one type of thinking—the tension you feel is simply a reflection of a busy mind.

And boy oh boy I totally get how busy it can be in there, and how life totally changes when we see we don't have to pay attention to any of it! What a relief it was for me.

Your mind clears of thought naturally on its own, and the presence of your urge is an invitation to step back, wait, and let your mind slow down.

Focus on your mind/body healing practices instead of that busy mind! Go through your doorway to peace.

Apparently, humans are the only creatures who speed up when we're lost. Other creatures stop and wait to regain their bearings. We rush forward, push through, speed up… thinking that doing more is where the answers lie.

But the answers always live in doing less. In slowing down, so we can hear our own guidance system speak… that beautiful thing we all have called wisdom.

When I deeply saw that my habit was nothing more than an innocent misunderstanding, I started to change my relationship to it. It was never about the thoughts that were coming up… it was always about my reaction to them. My deep fear that they were personal, all about me, and all about who I was as a human being. And that if I didn't obey them, my life would be under threat.

One thing I know for certain… it's never been about me at all. My character, my lack of willpower, my lack of 'something'.

The same is true for you.

It is a valuable warning sign that I'm super grateful I know about now.

Thirty

When we heal the inside, the outside comes along for the ride.

When I was 40 years old, I was overweight, tired, and on the path to type 2 diabetes. Now I am over 50 I am lean, fit, and have completely reversed prediabetes.

On the surface, the transformation looks totally physical.

But it is not.

The inside transformation has been far greater.

Nothing is as good, as healthy feels. At 40 I was insulin resistant, overweight, and tired all the time. It was a struggle to get through my days. I didn't like being this weight. I would be lying if I said I did!

But I've since learned that my body was protecting me.

It was doing all that it could to keep my body working. All I had to do, was acknowledge that and start to live in a way that allowed my body to stop doing those protective things, such as keep fat in storage while it constantly worked at getting my blood sugar down. I just had to change a few things and help it out.

Weight gain or weight loss is a side effect. I have worked with hundreds of people over the years, who have effortlessly experienced the weight loss side effect that happens when we give our bodies a break and realign with it.

Does it mean it's easy?

No.

Like most principles they are at on one level profoundly simple, yet difficult to implement.

I've made it my passion for over 10 years to look, learn and create ways to effectively help people successfully change their environments to their low carb lifestyle, and to heal.

While at the same time, learning to embrace the life we have now, love who we are, and to tap into the innate gifts that we all have.

None of that needs to wait a second longer than it has.

I know there's so much I haven't yet seen, and that excites me.

Because the minute I think I 'know' something?

That's the minute I stop learning.

Thirty One

There is power in the pause.

Pausing before you act can change everything, and there are a couple of ways we can pause.

The purposeful pause we can do when we notice we've moved from green to orange—we're heading down in a spiral or we notice we're already in the weeds. A conscious pause that allows insight into your thoughts and feelings and where they're directing you, and conscious pause to consider whether that's aligned with your direction and values or not.

And this pause can happen at any time. Before you act, or during the act. It's simply when you notice you are acting in a way you don't want to.

Just setting that intention is what matters. You won't always do it—perfection is never the goal—but to keep trying is what matters.

This intentional pause is what we generally do in the beginning when we're learning the truth about our habit. But once we start to see who we are that lives well beyond that, the pause may start to look different.

It's a little hard to explain in words how this happens, it's something you need to experience. But over time, as my understanding totally shifted from seeing my habitual thoughts as anything powerful or meaningful, my pause happened automatically.

Almost like it happened for me, rather than actively by me. Do you see how that could happen?

Seeing the urges as not 'me', not who I was, as simply thoughts I had repeatedly acted upon reoccurring, they just stopped feeling so compelling. The thought that I had to have that wine became something that I noticed briefly but could totally see I didn't have to grab.

Imagine your thoughts as like a bus coming through. Why would you hop on the one not taking you towards your destination? Not only that, would you hop on every bus that went past? How would you ever get anything else done, and how do you know where you will end up?

That's what it became like for me.

'Oh, here comes that bus again, but it's not my bus.'

It does become effortless when you see thought in this way. You just see the ones clearly you want to let pass by.

There are simply no 'pause' rules, and I've seen over the years it tends to naturally move from more conscious to more automatic. It will fluctuate constantly as you may slip into different habits without noticing… and then you do start to notice. Any type of pause that allows you to tap back into your inbuilt resources, to consider, to see your next move and ensure it aligns, is excellent.

All that matters really is that you create the space between 'you' and your habit… enough space to allow you to make sure you're getting on your bus that's going to take you where you want to go.

So, is what you're about to say or do, or is that ruminating thought going around in your head, your bus? Where are you headed by staying on that one?

Trust me… there are billions of other buses available to you… you just need to get off the one you're on.

Sending love.

Thirty Two

Living in the unknown.

We're living in a time of huge uncertainty, but is that any different to normal?

No, it's not. We are always living in the unknown.

We could never possibly know what the future holds, even though our minds love to fill our heads with stories and tell us we can predict the future.

But that security is an illusion.

Living through the years that were 2020 and 2021, it felt like we were thrust into a lot of unknowns about the future. But all that actually happened, was that we were made a lot more aware of the fact that we can never know what the future holds.

A level of acceptance around that allows us a bit of breathing space and helps to remove some of the anxiety around the fact that we can't predict the future.

The only thing we know for sure is this very present moment.

It looks very much like we are at the mercy of many others making decisions about our lives, but it always is like that.

It just feels a lot more intense right now.

On the days when I get caught up in my thinking that looks a lot like worry, depressed, pity party, angry, frustrated, eventually what happens is I get to the end of my rope, and something then naturally shifts. I eventually see my habitual thinking is just keeping me in a place I don't want to be in, and I shift my focus away from it.

I tune in more to my wisdom.

The habitual mind is very limited and is rarely where the answers to life's questions are found.

You can decide to step away from your habitual mind.

In fact, if you want to transform, evolve, and grow or find solutions to your worries, it is a fundamental requirement to do that.

Wherever you're sitting right now if you are feeling at the end of your rope, know that you've only reached the end of that limited small mind.

There is still so much more on offer and available to you when you can step away onto the edge of your habitual mind and become a passive observer.

Imagine your thinking as a tidal pool of water.

You can choose to either swim right in it against the current and push through all the sludge, or you can step away and allow space to open inside you for fresh thought, fresh possibilities, fresh solutions.

Which will you choose?

It's incredible to deeply know that we have a choice.

Thirty Three

Most of the shadows in life are caused by standing in our own sunshine.

Ralph Waldo Emerson

What do we need to see to overcome our limiting beliefs and grow?

The only thing in the way of this, is your awareness and understanding of how change actually works.

How do we learn?

One misunderstanding is, that we think our brain loves to learn.

But it absolutely doesn't love to learn.

It will try and sabotage your efforts to change in every way it can.

As we grow up, we form a set of beliefs and stories about who we are, what we're capable of, what's right, what's wrong based on everything that we interact with in our world.

What the brain tends then to do, it is set out confirming the beliefs that we have developed and interpreted from our unique experience within the world.

We look only to confirm what we already believe.

In a sense, our brain is belief blind.

Seeing this reality helps to overcome a lot of the feelings that typically accompany change. Of course, our brain is going to want us to stay the same!

Transformation then, really looks like a great unlearning.

Unlearning all the beliefs we have, that are keeping us from healing.

Our ability to change, evolve, grow, connect is sitting right in front of us, but we just can't see it.

All you need to do, is to start to understand this.

It's not about trying to uncover all the beliefs we have.

It's way simpler than that.

All you need to do is to start watching how quickly your brain is dismissing new information that comes your way.

And when it does that, instead of complying, step back to put it aside for a while.

You can grab a cup, let's call it a considering cup, and put in it all the beliefs that your brain quickly wants to dismiss.

Leave them there for a few days and see if they are

worth coming back to another time.

This at least gives you space to see whether it might actually be worth considering.

The other thing to realise about change, is that it is uncomfortable.

Growth never is anything but uncomfortable.

But so what?

Why does discomfort have to stop us from learning?

Why do we have to fear being uncomfortable when we know it's normal?

When we know it's only temporary?

When we know underneath it all… we're still okay?

Thirty Four

A change in our attitudes and behaviour is a very slow process that requires conscious and consistent effort.

We've become so used to the idea that much of what we don't like about ourselves, and our lives, can be quickly overcome with very little effort on our part. But a change in our attitudes and behaviour is a very slow process that requires conscious and consistent effort.

We can't work at it all the time, but we notice when we don't we drop back into auto pilot. We tend to see our old habits rise and take the lead. That's nothing to do with you, who you are, or any value judgement. That's about your humanness.

Examining your life and changing it for the better is a difficult process that requires you to take responsibility for your thoughts and feelings—deciding what you need to do or stop doing, then reflect that in your choices.

Wishes and intentions are not actually change.

A common illusion by those seeking to change their lives is that it can be rapidly achieved. Once we 'know' what to do, it appears that we simply ought to be able to do it.

The most familiar of our behaviours are the ones generally most resistant to change—drinking, eating processed junk, smoking, scrolling, porn, drugs, comfort.

Here we need to understand the psychological power of a habit. Some are ‘good’ and life enhancing—many are not and become so entrenched within our lives and entangled with who we are and how we cope with life.

It’s obvious to me that any process directed at changing, even just a little, our well-established patterns of thinking and behaving is going to be an extended one and will involve efforts at gaining insight, re-evaluating behaviours, and trying new approaches.

Under the best of circumstances, these changes take time.

To imagine that such traits can be changed overnight or as soon as we become aware of them is to discount the well-established strength of habits, and the slowness with which we translate new knowledge into behaviour.

When we think about things that alter our lives in a moment, nearly all are bad. Phone calls in the night, a diagnosis, loss of a job, loved ones passing. Apart from a last-minute goal or winning the lottery, it’s hard to imagine sudden good news.

Virtually all the happiness and healing processes in our lives take time, usually a long time. Learning new things, changing old behaviours, building satisfying relationships, healing from trauma, rebuilding your health.

This is why patience and determination are among life's primary virtues (which perhaps might be one of your core values?).

In a society based on consumption, instant gratification is pervasive. Somewhere along the line in our history we became impatient people, expecting quick answers to all difficulties.

But the process of building has always been slow. The tension between simplicity and effort works itself out in our daily lives. It takes time for us to notice and see that in any moment we can choose which path to take.

And if we believe in the sudden transformation illusion, we are less likely to pursue the harder and less immediately satisfying work of becoming the person we wish to be.

So, here's the role of time, patience, grit, and reflection in our lives. What we believe about how life works and our place in it will determine whether we can find a satisfying way to live through it.

There is much in here to contemplate and ask yourself what you believe.

Because what you believe becomes your reality.

Thirty Five

Today I needed to remind myself of what I know.

There's so much I don't know, but the little I do reminds me of my humanness, and the humanness of everyone else around me who are doing the best they can.

Everything passes.

Feelings are created within me. I don't have to judge them or will them away, they will leave when my thinking changes (which it will, like the weather changes).

We only have the present moment.

I am free to express my own opinions, and so is everyone else.

I don't need anyone else to agree with me, to validate my own view.

My view is a product of my own thought system which means it will be limited by what I've seen, heard, experienced, and believe. So is everyone else's.

This makes it *my* reality, but not *reality.*

Change happens when we transcend our beliefs and look to learn beyond them.

If my opinion differs from yours, it's not about you. It's not personal. It doesn't make you wrong, it doesn't make me right. It just is that way because of the way humans work. We can choose to be offended… or curious.

This isn't a dress rehearsal.

The journey is in the experience.

Joy lives there too.

I operate from either love or fear. Fear is limited and is a mental prison. Love is limitless and creates freedom. I always have a choice.

My first reaction to my thinking is not usually my best. Creating space between the thought and the reaction gives me more choice.

I am enough now.

When I feel the urge to change my external environment, it's my wisdom telling me to look within.

I may not agree with and like what others say, but I respect their right to say it.

Thirty Six

Resilience (noun)
The ability to recover quickly from illness, change, or misfortune; buoyancy.
The act of springing back, rebounding, or resiling.
The American Heritage® Dictionary of the English Language, 5th Edition

The ability to stand up after you get knocked down.

Do you know it is already within you?

We are born with an innate resilience. With everything we need.

You just need to spend time in nature to see how every animal, plant, living creature know how to live. They have an innate intelligence within.

So do we.

The problem is, while we're born with what we need to navigate our way through life, our inbuilt GPS system, we're also born with an ability to convince us of the opposite.

Our psychology loves to get in the way and tricks us in to thinking that we are broken.

A huge part of transformation is reconnecting with what is innate within.

No one or anything can take that away.

This doesn't mean horrible things don't happen to people.

They of course do.

But the impact what happens to us is largely dictated by the thinking that we keep hold of about these events.

Our psychology is what we learn here.

It isn't who we are.

Simply knowing that is enough to start breaking the foundations of those beliefs that have held us in place for so long.

What are the signs of wellbeing in humans?

Security.

Flow.

Love.

Wisdom.

Confidence.

Kindness.

Compassion.

These are things we don't have to learn.

They are simply things we need to reconnect with, within us.

Stepping out of your head and back in the present moment of your reality will help you to do that.

Are you in your head? Or in your life?

It really is your choice to make.

Thirty Seven

Are you still here with me?

How are you at surfing?

I used to be a terrible surfer. I used to fall off and cry, take so long to get back up, lie down and get smashed by another wave before I had even a chance to stand.

But I'm pretty good at it now… a surfer of life I mean.

In life, we all experience highs and lows, ups and downs, just like the waves on the ocean.

Sometimes the ocean is calm, and it's an effortless flow, sometimes it's so rough and choppy that it creates a lot of turmoil.

From this perspective in the ocean, it looks like chaos, it looks like unpredictability. But if we can shift our gaze just a little bit deeper, we will see that the ocean is calm, quiet, and peaceful.

So, where do you believe you live?

If you believe, like I used to, that life is only found in the waves of your day-to-day experience, then you will be tossed around like a buoy.

Continually at the mercy of the circumstances happening outside of you.

Or… can you get a glimpse of that calm world that lives just beneath your experience?

There's no way we can't be tossed around by the waves if we're human.

I just don't try to control my experience anymore.

And I'm way better at surfing the waves now.

However, I am feeling in any moment is what I'm feeling.

It is transient, like the stormy ocean.

It will pass.

I do what I see to do, which yesterday looked to me like a nap on my daughter's couch.

When we know where our experience comes from, we don't have to fear the ocean.

We can let go of trying to harness something that's impossible to control, and just continually improve surfing the waves of life.

Thirty Eight

How you show up to life is always up to you.

The external contents of our world are always in flux. Life will continue to throw curve balls, unexpected events, unexpected happenings every single day.

It has always been like that and always will continue like that. And the majority of that isn't in our control (even though we like to think it is and we spend a lot of energy trying to make it true).

What we get to decide is what we bring to the table. Our reaction and our attitude… the way we see what's being thrown our way.

That is always our responsibility and all that we truly can ever control.

The essence of healing is in seeing this and creating the opportunities to see more choice where we don't see we have choice, and then accepting and releasing that which we cannot change.

How do we do this?

By noticing. By slowing down. By becoming more aware of our thoughts and feelings. By releasing others to be responsible for their own thoughts and feelings.

By deeply seeing that we're only ever in control of what we bring to any situation in our life.

The rest is not up to us.

Thirty Nine

Your light within really does light up the world.

This is what is so beautiful about the work you are doing my friend. You are turning on your inner light for the world to see, so that others may then follow your light. The more you light this up within yourself, the message to others is that they have this too. They too can light themselves up from within.

In my work I am blessed to mentor other coaches. Our work together is all about helping them light that spark within so they can then help others. This is how we change the world. One light at a time.

I can only see what's in you, when I can see what's in me. It all starts from within, but there is no limits as to where it ends.

Forty

I think it's time you met our OWL. She can be your guide on this inner journey.

The OWL. She is like you. Wise, strong, and can see in many directions.

The OWL. She is here to guide you to your inner wisdom. She is a beautiful metaphor to help you make more heart centred choices that align with your values, rather than subconscious habitual ones.

The **O** in *O*WL, is where we start. In the **observations.** Noticing, observing.

As an adult, we often speed through life without much observation of our patterns, reactions, inner world, expectations, judgements, choices.

Without observation and which gives us awareness, we can't start to make a different choice.

This is particularly relevant when it comes to patterns in our life that hurt us (or others) whether that is physical, emotional, short- or long-term damage.

There isn't much we need to do when it comes to observation. We only need to slow down, and look. Sounds easy, but for most of us, it's not.

Most of us never consciously slow down for fear of what we might see. What if we see something we don't like? What if there is more 'work' for me to do? What if I experience uncomfortable feelings? What then? What would I do? What if I get bored? Imagine if I got bored and didn't have anything to do.

None of that is likely to be a conscious thought.

But your body knows it all. You are just not tuned in to it. None of us really are. But we continue to ignore it at our own risk.

Change requires you to show up to yourself, and to your life, every single day.

O**W**L is to be **willing**. Willing to do what it takes, face your fears, sit in discomfort, confront your choices, and be willing to make a different one that will take you towards the life you're wanting. If we're not willing, nothing will change.

OW**L** is in **living your values.** Your inner values will allow you to feel like you're inputting the coordinates to your own GPS. Values can be hard to become conscious of because most of what we think we value isn't really ours. It's conditioned from outside of ourselves.

Values are the qualities we want to bring to how we treat ourselves (first and foremost), and others. Clarity with values comes when we ask ourselves how we would like others to describe us.

To observe and be willing are the two most essential requirements of change.

Forty One

I honour the place in you where the entire universe resides. I honour the place in you of love, of truth, of peace, and of light. And when you are in that place in you and I am in that place in me, there is only one of us. A definition of the word Namaste.

Connection.

Does anything else matter as much as connecting with other human beings?

It is truly inbuilt in all of us. We are hardwired to connect with others.

While it seems like something that must be learnt; the reality is all we need to do is unlearn all the layers we have built in our minds that get in the way of our natural ability to connect.

Have you ever been at a conference or a function where you've connected with the people there so well, that at the end of the conference you've wanted to exchange numbers because you have felt such a deep connection?

I used to think that this only happened on very rare occasions.

However, the reality is that ability to connect at that deep level with anybody is possible when we step out of our psychology and step into the present moment.

The judgements, the insecure thinking, the stories. Paying attention to those, blocks any connection.

Stepping away from those thoughts and shifting focus to the now, creates the possibility for a deep connection with anyone.

Human to human.

Soul to soul.

Why wouldn’t you want to do more of that?

Forty Two

I do what I do, not because there's somewhere better, I need to be. I do what I do to experience the juice of everything that is right in front of me, right now.

There's nothing you have to be, do, change or have to experience 'life' in this very present moment.

I used to believe I was inadequate unless I kept learning, growing, was more disciplined, wasn't lazy, looked a certain way, did more.

Oh wow, how life has changed for me now I've seen through that illusion.

It was my belief of those illusions that kept me from seeing I was fine, just as I was.

I have this discussion often with clients, and I get back very often, 'but if I accept who I am today, won't that mean I will never lose weight or get healthy?'

Again, another illusion.

Consider these questions.

Can you change the past?

What if you knew you always did the best you could in any moment, given the thinking that you had at the time?

How would you see your past given that fact?

What if you deeply believed you are not your choices?

That in fact, who you are goes far greater and deeper than that?

What if all you had to see, is that you only needed to 'see' more to be able to increase your ability to make different choices?

How would life change today, right now for you, if you could see that focussing on the past or some predicted future was only sucking the energy out of life in this present moment?

Acceptance of you, including everything about your past is a vital part in moving forward.

It frees you from a whole lot of mental clutter that's sapping your energy to focus on today.

Because today is all you have.

It's all we ever have.

Which means, you are free to choose to do anything you want to do today, regardless of the decisions and choices you made yesterday, last week, last year or 10 years ago.

Acceptance is freedom.

Acceptance is love.

Accept your perfectly imperfect self, and you will also accept the imperfections in others.

Forty Three

The emotional terrain we sit in, is a very important driver when it comes to the quality of our health.

The thinking we sit in, is felt through our entire body. This is why the feeling of stress is actually a feeling of thought.

Over time, it can become a trigger for many health conditions, like autoimmune diseases.

For most people, their tolerance to stress is way too high.

They are sitting in a constant underlying elevated stress level from overthinking, rushing, over analysing, perfectionism, and more.

This is what needs addressing, from the inside out.

It's a huge piece of the puzzle, and it's what most people avoid.

But if we're brave and we do it, the magic happens.

It is so important to understand that the weather you sit in comes from thought.

While it looks like everything we feel is coming from the world outside of us; it never is.

It can only ever come from the thinking we have about the world outside of us.

Our ability to deal with and bounce back from acute events is dependent on our understanding of where our experience of life is coming from, and whether our nervous system is resilient.

If we've been sitting in higher levels of everyday stress for long periods of time, it's not likely to be easy to bounce back.

But all that can change, simply by tuning in more to your body, and listening to the love notes it is sending you.

Start observing your feelings of your body.

Stress in and of itself, is a feeling.

It is a feeling that is internally created.

Notice when you feel stressed, where is your mind?

Don't simply hop on that train and let your mind take you where it wants.

You are not at the mercy of your thinking.

Your thinking is rarely telling you anything that is important, yet your body always is.

Your body's wisdom is incredible.

It will tell you when you're up in your mind and it's time to step away.

It is time to pay more attention to your body, rather than the spinning wheel of your mind.

Forty Four

Successful people have just learned to not be stopped by their doubts and fears.

Just a reminder that everyone experiences these feelings.

Not just you!

And sometimes when we do, we want to run away.

I've wanted to do that many times in my life, and have done that many times when it felt uncomfortable, or it looked like I might fail… or succeed!

But I've seen that the only difference between someone who achieves what they want in life, and those who don't, is the running away part.

Feelings don't need to determine whether we move forward in life or not.

We are meant to feel all the feels in life.

I love that about life now that I see this!

But feelings can only dictate our path if we choose to let them.

Feelings are just thoughts in the moment.

When we spend time becoming more aware of that we will usually see when we don't feel good, it's because our thinking is taking us on a ride and is making up a whole bunch of stories we're believing. Lots of ifs, buts and maybes.

How could we possibly know?

We only limit ourselves by guessing.

You have an innate capacity to thrive.

It is your true nature.

What ultimately influences your sense of fulfilment, connection, motivation, and your ability to flourish, is how you think life works.

How do you think life works?

Forty Five

As you connect more deeply with that innate essence in you, change will be inevitable.

Change is so much easier from a place of love.

I often say to my clients that self-love is the magic ingredient of growth, transformation, and positive health changes.

Many find this hard to understand, because the feeling is, that if I accept where I am today, I won't want to change.

That is a fundamental misunderstanding.

The opposite is true.

Accepting where you are today is simply the most loving and compassionate thing you can do.

Every decision you have ever made up to this point in your life has been because it's the best decision you've seen to do in that moment.

Does it mean it's the best for you going into the future? Not always, but in the moment, you made your choice,

Your past does not have to define you in any way unless you let it. You can release yourself from the burdens you carry from your past choices that are weighing you down.

In fact, it is the only way to move forward and free yourself.

You can mark a line in the sand today.

Yesterday has gone, tomorrow hasn't happened, all you have is today.

If you choose to see you have many options available to you in any given moment, they will find you.

You don't have to choose the same ones you always have.

You really don't.

Thank them and send them on their way if they no longer serve you.

There is a buffet of choice available, you just need to wait for it to come to you.

Forty Six

My definition of confidence? Showing up as yourself with your heart wide open.

Want to have more confidence to live the life you want?

Then read on.

Consider this question.

What is the opposite of confidence?

Self-doubt? Anxiety? Shyness? Insecure? Introvert?

What if the opposite to confidence was none of those.

What if the opposite to confidence was self-conscious?

What I've realised in recent years, is when I'm feeling most confident, there is one thing not on my mind.

Me.

I'm not thinking about myself.

When I'm feeling most confident my thoughts are focused on anything other than me.

When I'm feeling self-conscious, which looks like a whole of stuff I have lacking within, my thoughts are focused on me. What others will think of me, how I look, how I sound, whether I know enough, whether I'm good enough, whether I am as good as her… you get the drill.

We all do it.

But we should stop, if we want to suck the juice out of life.

So, you see, we're all confident. And all that's getting in the way is a whole lot of thought.

Dropping all those unhelpful stories in my own head, was what finally propelled me to do the things I wanted to do in my life.

What a joke to think we are not born with all these innate gifts to flourish in life!

When you're not feeling confident, where is your focus?

On you, or on them?

Transform your life by dropping all those stories you have, about who you are and what you're capable of.

Give it a try and tell me what you see.

Forty Seven

Affirmations without understanding are just another layer on top of misunderstanding. You would never build a house on poor foundations, would you?

Today while I was with a client, I talked about how important it was to know that underneath all our psychology is our true nature of wellbeing.

To really find peace and heal from our past experiences, we need to know deeply who we really are.

We need to stop running away from ourselves through our behaviours and learn to sit with our fears, our discomforts, our joys.

Unless we do that, healing looks like more layers upon a very rocky foundation.

And who are you?

An interesting question many will search a lifetime to try and answer.

But I've seen it's quite simple.

Who are you when there isn't much on your mind?

When you're present in the moment, when your mind is still and quiet?

If you reflect to a time when you did that, you will feel it.

You know it.

So often we miss it because we're not tuned in to the present moment, instead we're tuned in to the noise of our thinking.

We create complex routines, we're busy, we do many things to escape the present moment.

Healing is really the great unlearning. It is peeling off the band-aids we have innocently covered ourselves with over our lifetime, to protect ourselves.

You don't need those protections, thank you. Certainly not the protections our little mind has to offer.

What you need to do is return home. Return to your body and sit with all that comes up with you.

No more running. No more mindless numbing.

Only then will we heal and see the protective layers come off one at a time.

Then we will have returned.

Are you ready?

Home is calling you.

Listen.

You will hear.

Forty Eight

I believe insulin resistance is the single most common health disorder in the world. It will increase the risk of every chronic disease.

Dr Ben Bikman

Understanding insulin resistance, and how to avoid it, is vital for your health.

It is the precursor to the majority of modern diseases in the world today.

If you are insulin resistant, you are at risk of developing a range of diseases, including metabolic syndrome, high blood pressure, type 2 diabetes, cardiovascular disease, cancer, neurological disease, and for women, polycystic ovary syndrome (PCOS).

Insulin is a hormone secreted by the pancreas, which sits in the abdomen. When we eat food that is a carbohydrate, that carbohydrate is broken down into glucose in the gut and absorbed into the bloodstream.

That's when insulin gets to work. Its role is varied, but one of its main roles is to move the glucose out of the blood and into the tissuesand the muscles where it can be stored as glycogen, the body's storage form for carbohydrates, for later use as a fuel.

Once the storage capacity for glycogen in the liver and muscles is complete, insulin takes the excess glucose to the liver, where it is converted into fat, known as fatty liver.

That fat will only be mobilised for fuel when insulin levels drop. This is why insulin is called our 'fat storage hormone.'

In a normal system, insulin and glucose levels drop after the glucose from a meal has been absorbed into the tissues, the body responds by feeling hungry and the brain tells us to eat again.

This is the well-known blood glucose rollercoaster.

When the diet is consistently high in carbohydrates, in the form of sugar or other carbs such as starches or grains, the level of insulin in the blood remains elevated.

This is known as a condition called hyperinsulinemia, and leads to a number of issues, including storage of excess carbs as fat, prevention of the breakdown of fat when we need fuel, and insulin resistance.

Be informed and learn about this condition that is preventable and such a factor in health.

Signs of insulin resistance are many, but include belly fat, high blood pressure, uncontrolled blood glucose, high insulin, high triglycerides, fatty liver, poor energy, skin tags, erectile dysfunction, brain fog, irregular or painful periods, dark skin patches.

If you want a good book to read to understand this even further, and what to do about it, I highly recommend Dr Peter Brukner's book, *A Fat Lot of Good.*

There are many doctors and researchers speaking out about this. Do your research. Don't just believe the headlines.

Forty Nine

Whatever you think, well, you're probably right.

.

What is something that you really want to do in your life but just haven't done it.

Get healthy? Run a marathon? Write a book? Create a business? Learn to sing?

Sit in some quiet space inside and listen to what this might be for you.

Now, ask yourself, what is stopping you from achieving it?

Most of the time we have a deep knowing in our soul, that says we want to do something in our life.

But how many never do it?

Not because of talent, lacking discipline or lacking motivation.

But because we listen to those voices in our head that talk us out of it.

Tell us we can't, we might fail, we might look stupid,

we don't have enough knowledge, we don't have enough money, it will be hard…

There could be a million reasons not to do it.

And if you keep listening to those voices, you never will do it.

And one day you will get to a point in your life that you will look back with a sigh and say to yourself how much you wished you had just done it.

Life is not a dress rehearsal!

You've only got this one shot.

The voice may be saying, oh but you've got plenty of time.

That's the biggest lie of all.

'The trouble is, you think you have time.' Buddha.

You don't. You only have today, no one knows what tomorrow will bring.

You don't have to be a slave to those voices in your head. They are not you.

You are simply the one who hears them. You can stop listening to them anytime you want. They're not keeping you safe, they're keeping you small.

Those voices don't have any idea of your capabilities. So, stop limiting yourself by guessing.

What is that thing you've always wanted to do?

Just. Do. It.

No matter what happens, you will be okay.

Fifty

Self-care isn't bubble baths and champagne. It's alignment. Alignment between who you are at your core, and the daily choices you make.

Is self-care an area you need to give more focus to? It's not selfish to care for yourself. It's essential. As women and mothers, we often put ourselves behind everyone else. But should we? If we don't look after ourselves, are we not risking it all?

In my eyes, self-care is about taking responsibility for yourself. Knowing your values, your needs, and ensuring they are met. This isn't about manipulating others to give you what you need. It's about dedicating the space to give this to yourself.

Fifty One

Metabolism is your bodies powerhouse. Metabolic health is the performance of your powerhouse.

Have you ever heard of the words 'metabolism' and 'metabolic health' before? If you haven't, please read on. Knowing and understanding these terms are super important for overall health, wellbeing, and longevity.

You may have used the term metabolism before. Often, we hear people say, 'I have a slow metabolism.' This isn't really true. No one is born with a slow metabolism. But during life in the modern world with all the toxic inputs we unintentionally (and intentionally) put into our bodies, along with a overly sedentary lifestyle, over time, our metabolic health can be negatively impacted. This means we may experience low energy, brain fog, poor sleep, irritability, depression, anxiety, and many of the modern-day diseases we are seeing today.

But with understanding, we can do what we need to do to support our own metabolic health! Type 2 diabetes for example, which you know I was on my way towards, is a sign that my metabolic health was not working as it should. When I changed the inputs—my diet, my lifestyle, and did the inner work, I was able to fix it. So many conditions people experience today are a function of poor metabolic health, but they can be fixed if we treat the root cause, and we get to it early.

Metabolic health is essential to mental health. The connection between our metabolic health and mental health is very well known. Yet the mental health space is largely blind to this importance. If you would like to read a great book on the link between metabolic health and mental health, I highly recommend *Change Your Diet, Change Your Mind* by psychiatrist, Dr Georgia Ede.

Metabolism is how your brain and body make and use energy to keep you going. We know food is a huge player here, but also electron currency. Metabolic health is about how well this system works. Metabolism is the petrol I guess, and metabolic health is the engine. If the petrol is dirty or poor or the engine doesn't work well, there will be problems.

Change can be virtually impossible if your mind and body doesn't have the energy needed to assist you. If your metabolic health isn't where it should be, how much energy is your body going to give you to cover the energy expensive change process? I truly believe that most people don't change because of this reason. Even when they learn what they can do, if they aren't firing on all cylinders, it can be impossible to do what you know you need to do.

Insulin resistance is closely linked to metabolic health, and it is a serious metabolic disorder that is reaching epidemic proportions in many places around the world. Bombarding the brain with too much insulin can lead to insulin resistance, making it difficult for the insulin to enter the brain, which is needed to help turn glucose into energy.

When there is insulin resistance within the brain, insulin can't cross the blood/brain barrier. Glucose still can enter the brain, but this glucose is largely useless without the insulin to utilize that energy. So essentially the brain is starving in a sea of glucose.

You can control your glucose and insulin levels by changing what you eat.

There is no doubt that this is the number one mechanism to remain (or return) to insulin sensitivity which is the opposite of insulin resistance.

Good metabolic health means your energy production is getting you through your day. Large spikes in blood sugar and insulin levels lead to insulin resistance over time, which damages your whole metabolism, chipping away at your mental and physical health.

Food choices are your metabolism game changer. This is where you have a great deal of power. By fine-tuning your food choices, you can dramatically improve your metabolic health and your brain performance within a matter of weeks.

The business of big food has really made knowing what to eat difficult. Processed foods are sold as superfoods, and foods we've evolved on over our entire human existence have been wrongly vilified with no science behind it. What you eat is powerful. It is either helping you maintain a working metabolic system and keeping you free of disease, or it's slowly making you tired, slow, and lacking in energy.

I am well studied in nutrition. But not the nutrition that has been behind the big food backed food pyramid. When I followed that, I got sick. When I started to investigate where I was going wrong, I found people like Mark Sisson, Gary Taubes, Nina Teicholz, Dr Peter Brukner, and Prof Tim Noakes. I have studied extensively through the Nutrition Network and and have taught within many of their programs over the years.

So, what should you eat?

Real food. Minimally processed foods that are naturally high in beautiful animal fats (the only plant fats I eat are coconut oil or olive oil). The other fats like canola oil, vegetable oil, seed oils are toxic to our bodies. And yet, they are in virtually every food you buy in the supermarket.

Eat real food. Don't avoid the foods we evolved to eat; animal foods are superior in terms of energy content and nutritional value. Focus on eating animal protein, beautiful animal fats, and keep your processed carbohydrates and processed foods to a minimum.

Much of what is in our 'food' environment today isn't really food. It is a concoction of chemicals. Is it any wonder why we are getting so sick in mind and body with what we're we eat?

Our brain needs to recognise what we eat so it knows what to do with it. Food is information, and most modern-day foods have lost this information. This causes chaos in the body, and chaos causes inflammation.

Over time, we risk poor metabolic health and the consequences that stem from that.

If you have never thought about what you're putting in your body, don't wait till you get a diagnosis to do it. Do it now. The sooner you do, the better you will feel, and the more likely you will be to avoid that diagnosis in the first place.

And… you will give yourself that beautiful brain energy you need to change your life, from the inside out.

Fifty Two

Stop expecting new results from old, repeated behaviours.

This is not a character flaw when we do this, and it's so, so common. I used to think it was all about me lacking something, or I simply wasn't trying hard enough.

But that's not it.

It's just that we lack the awareness we need to see something new.

A habit is just a thought… without any reflection.

So where does our behaviour come from in the first place?

It is the invisible pull from within that guide everything we do. To the extent that we understand that our experience is created from within us, is the extent to which we will be able to see beyond our habitual thinking.

Change can happen but it starts from within you.

It takes awareness, patience and commitment.

A deep knowing that all behaviours come from thought, your own thought, not someone else's.

You can't change the thinking that comes in, but you can decide what you want to focus on and what you will do with it.

If you keep focusing on the same thinking, then nothing will change.

How deeply do you want to see beyond the behaviours that are not serving you?

Spend some time reflecting on that and create space between your thoughts and your reaction.

This creates insight and insight leads to change.

Fifty Three

I've learned when I'm in a low mood, not to trust the way I see myself.

My growth and understanding around this has been dramatic over the last few years. Mostly, because I didn't even know I couldn't ever trust my thinking.

I thought because I was thinking it, it meant it required my attention. Often it demanded my attention, and I spent so much time in conversation with my thoughts.

But seeing I wasn't the thinker, I was just the one who was hearing it, changed my life.

Especially when it came to moods.

Not only should you not trust the way you see yourself when you're in a low mood, but you should just have a general suspicion about the way you see everything when you're looking through the foggy lens of a low mood.

The same situation looks very different depending on the mood we're in.

It's not the situation; it's the lens we're seeing it through.

When we're in a bad mood we usually become reactive. We blame others, we spew our inner world on to our outer world, we get annoyed easily. We often say and do things we later regret.

Until we see that when we're in a low mood, it's unwise to trust our thinking.

When we become sceptical, we see it's probably not a good idea to act.

Have you ever noticed how much you're in your thoughts when you're in a low mood? The temptation to get in there to try to solve and fix it innocently creates more mess you must wade through.

What if instead of jumping in, instead you put it down and left it alone?

Everyone experiences low moods.

Whether they impact our lives or not comes down to the level of awareness we have of whether we should trust our thinking in these times… or leave it be.

Start to get curious. Where are you when you're in a low mood?

Now you also understand how food can affect mood, can you start to see that when you eat processed foods, your mood is also affected? What might change if the next few meals where real nutrient dense home cooked foods? What about if you try it for a week or two?

It is very powerful to consciously make that connection between what you eat and how you feel.

Start to notice. See what you see. And get curious enough to experiment for yourself.

Eating well may not solve all of your problems, but your thinking will radically improve when your brain is well nourished.

Fifty Four

What is the difference between someone who reaches their goals, and someone who doesn't?

What is 'motivation'?

Most people would say it is a feeling 'to do' something. It looks easy when we're feeling good, hard when we're not. It seems to come and go, wax and wane, and while we generally start anything we do with the best of intentions, often when the feeling of 'motivation' leaves us, we're at a loss as to what to do. We're filled with habitual thoughts that reflect beliefs around lack of discipline, unworthiness, our inability to do anything… all unhelpful thoughts I have already shown are not worthy of your attention.

What if a better way to think of 'motivation', is to understand that it will always be temporary, and rather that waiting for a certain feeling to come before you act, you decide you can just act anyway? This is where I teach my clients to focus on their plan, not their mood.

Moods are a part of normal human behaviour. They go up and down, changing like the weather.

How caught up in your own mood you get, will determine your ease of flow through your day… and your level of motivation to get things done.

Do you totally believe your thoughts from a place of a low mood? OR…?

Are you able to observe, stand back, get curious… without being drawn in and take action anyway? Nothing moves a mood along faster than some sort of action. Going for a walk, doing a gym session, sitting in the sun.

In low moods, our habitual mind is loud, bossy, and it doesn't want us to change.

How much we are impacted by this natural ebb and flow of our state of mind in any moment, is going to come down to our understanding of where our experience of life is coming from, and the fact that most of what we 'think' is totally optional.

When we want to change our behaviour, we must focus on new thinking. Not the old, stale habitual thinking that has kept you doing the same things over and over.

It's so important to understand what drives our behaviour if we want to change it.

But what drives behaviour is largely invisible to most people.

We are always driven to act from thought in the moment. Always, no exception. Thought leads to a feeling which leads to behaviour, which leads to a result.

How often have you paid attention to the thought feeling behaviour connection?

If you're anything like me, I had no awareness of this… until I did. But once you start to become aware of it, you will start to notice this connection and wake a lot more up to your experience of life.

To be able to change behaviour, we must create space between your reaction and the habitual mind which is where all your habitual thinking sits.

Seeing yourself as separate from this habitual, mostly unhelpful, brain junk is the key to behaviour change.

But you don't need to get busy on changing your thoughts. It's way easier than that.

All we need to see is that we can 'opt out' of the unhelpful thinking. And you will know this thinking because it doesn't feel good, it's often the same thoughts that go around and around, and they are very bossy, loud and strong, like your life depends on your attention to it.

When we're trying to stay motivated and change our behaviour, it is these old, familiar, and habitual thoughts that return which gets in our way most.

We believe them, we follow them, and motivation looks lost.

The difference between someone who appears totally motivated in life and someone who appears to not be motivated is simply the thinking they pay attention too.

Fifty Five

For many years I couldn't imagine that I could possibly get through raising my young children without alcohol helping me to relax at the end of a 'stressful' day.

In a podcast interview I gave recently; I was reminded how much I used to believe that food and alcohol were the tools I needed to help me navigate my life.

For many years I couldn't imagine that I could possibly get through raising my young children without alcohol helping me to relax at the end of a 'stressful' day. I also couldn't imagine ever seeing through the belief that I just had to eat certain foods because of the relief they brought. I reacted instantly to my internal emotions—to what life was throwing up.

I didn't question them; I just did whatever I saw to do to bring relief from what I was living in.

That relief lived in food and alcohol. For others it lives in complex daily routines and a myriad of other habits our mind has so helpfully created for us for us to be able to navigate life.

What started to gift me with the freedom from all my habits I didn't want any more was to see that these things didn't give me anything I had thought they did. They promised so much but never delivered on that promise.

I had to step back from the specific habit I wanted to stop and see that all feeling was energy created in the moment, and none of it I had to fear. I certainly didn't need to stop feeling it by acting on the urge. I just had to see it as the energy of a busy mind passing through me, and as soon as I did that, it was on its way out, and I got on with my day.

None of the things I did habitually—drinking, overeating, eating when I wasn't hungry—ever brought me pleasure. They're not things we innately want to do. I remember that first glass of alcohol and it was disgusting. And yes, perhaps a little bit of chocolate was pleasurable for a moment, but a whole block never was.

My mind had many stories attached to both food and alcohol that stopped me for so long from seeing what those habits were. My response to a habitual feeling that I didn't see couldn't be true, and if I didn't act, it would simply become too unbearable.

We have a massive capacity to see we are 'ok' in any experience. To see who we truly are, no matter what is coming through us.

When we know who we are and that we don't need anything externally to give or take us away from any feeling, we can start to see our habits from a different viewing point. We can expand our vision and awareness.

Life was simply better without alcohol and eating a

whole pile of junk food.

I did for a few years have a story I didn't see for a while about socially drinking and eating junk being something I wanted to be able to do (probably in order to fit in and not have to experience the uncomfortable feelings that often arise from standing out).

But I eventually saw through those ones too. Especially when I took a hard look at myself in the mirror and saw that socially drinking meant five or six glasses of champagne.

I was okay no matter what story my mind was spinning, which was constantly searching for ways I could moderate my habit. Perhaps I could have a binge on ice cream and chips every now and again. Or perhaps I could still drink socially when I wanted.

Well perhaps I could have if I had wanted to, but none of those things do anything for me, so I just don't want to do it. No willpower required. I just needed to remember who I am when I notice what old stories my mind is spinning.

That's what I deeply saw.

Why would I want to entertain and engage in ways I could moderate something that just never gave me anything I thought it did?

It's all a made-up story. All of it.

Your job is simply a remembering of who you deeply are.

Fifty Six

Owls. They are such beautiful birds. We often consider owls to be wise, they seem to have eyes that look right into our soul.

Can you imagine ever thinking that this animal wasn't good enough?

That it had come into this world lacking anything it needed to thrive or survive?

That it had to achieve a certain place in life, be of a certain weight, have the right house, job, car, or bank balance to be worthy enough to be here?

We would laugh at such a notion would we not! And yet, humans are a part of nature too, and we do this to ourselves all the time.

I love watching nature with my boys and marvelling at the incredible inbuilt capacity every creature on earth has to survive.

How they adapt, their resilience, their inbuilt GPS that guides them in life.

When I show my boys this, I am showing them that

same inbuilt capacity, is within them too. In all of us as humans. We are a part of nature… whether we feel connected with it or not.

And when you are pointed in this direction, you will start to see it everywhere.

We are not our experiences, our accomplishments, our failures, our successes, we most certainly are not our weight or our habits.

Who we are goes way beyond anything that our psychology could ever be. All those stories we have of ourselves, they're just made up.

Just like this beautiful bird, we too are wise. We have wisdom in abundance. We just need to look in the right direction for it. Nothing else is required.

Fifty Seven

What is the purpose of life?

To give?

To express our authentic self?

To create around us what drives and excites us, which in turn drives and excites others to do the same?

To tune out to the endless mindless chatter and return home to our body?

Have you ever paused and asked yourself this question?

If you haven't, why wouldn't you?

Life without a purpose doesn't seem like living to me.

And with your one life, why wouldn't you want to thrive, not just survive?

Fifty Eight

I don't approve of your lifestyle.
My lifestyle doesn't need your approval.

Have you experienced this from others?

When we appear to be stepping outside the 'norm', it can trigger comments like this in others.

Your lifestyle doesn't need anyone's approval except your own.

Indeed, no part of you or your choices needs the approval of others.

Be true to your heart.

If you are used to seeking approval from others for your own life, starting to unravel that within you will feel very uncomfortable.

Don't fear the discomfort. This is where growth happens.

It won't feel uncomfortable forever, but it will initially.

You're still okay. Keep going.

Fifty Nine

The wisdom in worry. There is wisdom in worry? That makes me worried!

We tend to worry a lot. About our kids, about our health, about whether it will work, about many things. Worrying is another job our mind likes to have.

I don't often remember lines from movies, but one line from the movie Bridge of Spies with Tom Hanks was memorable for me.

When a man is arrested and accused of being a Russian spy, his calm demeanour never changes. Tom as his lawyer trying to prevent him from being executed, asks him a couple of times during the movie, 'Aren't you worried?' To which the man replies, 'Would it help?'

What a great question, and one we can ask ourselves when we notice our mind busy worrying a lot… does it help?

Worry is a natural result of evolution. When our very distant relatives felt fear of an immediate threat, they took protective action, which was rewarded with surviving into the next moment. Apparently, scientists call this an 'immediate return' environment.

We know our brains haven't changed in the past 2000 years, but of course our environment has, and we now live in what's termed a 'delayed return' environment. There are very few immediate threats to our survival, and most of what we do (shopping, cooking, working) has a delayed return. They don't result in an immediate payoff, and it's not about immediate life or death.

Because of this, we have a bit of a mismatch going on. Our brain still behaves as though you might starve to death or be eaten by a lion at any moment—even though you have a cupboard full of food, and you only see lions in the zoo.

When your mind screams fear today, it's almost never in response to true danger. And because there is no immediate action for you to take (run or fight), the fear doesn't just rise and leave quickly, because there's simply nothing in front of you to immediately protect yourself from.

And here then comes worry.

What does your mind do? Jumps to interpreting fear in other ways, by imagining what might go wrong… which we all know, our minds just simply have no trouble filling in all the blanks.

Oh, how it loves a job to do. Minds hate uncertainty, so it will just spit out whatever it can to provide possibilities, most of which aren't accurate.

The evolutionary and adaptive lifesaving feeling

of fear that kept our ancestors alive in their immediate return environment looks like chronic anxiety and worry about things that aren't real in today's relatively safe world. Our minds spin stories full of details and emotion, and before long it looks like an inevitable reality. It creates a state of mind that makes it look so likely that those worries will come true.

Minds create our reality, and then say, 'I didn't do it.' It constantly pulls in evidence as proof of the stories it spins.

Here's the thing. If what happens in your world is something that your mind has said might, it won't have been because your mind knew it.

Life doesn't work in that way. Life only ever unfolds moment to moment… there's only now. And a mind, right now, creating stories and images and projecting them outwards into the world.

But they are not 'real things.'

They are thoughts.

I realised as a champion worrier from a very young age worrying that my parents would never come home when they went out, that worrying had become such a part of my experience. And often I wasn't consciously aware of the thoughts.

But oh, my wise body was telling me what my mind was up to. I felt it. And when I started understanding this wisdom, I started to pay more attention (that traffic light system), and step back. This stepping back gave me some much needed 'psychological space' to assess the situation beyond the narrow limits of my fearful mind.

Worry is such a mask we wear. We mistake it for love, and it makes life look so much more confusing and complicated than it really is.

We think it's helpful because it 'prepares us' to solve real problems. But does it?

Everything a mind does is to help you survive. And our brain's negativity bias and constant predictions for our survival as a species… but worry is like a rocking chair. It gives your mind something to do, but it takes you nowhere except out of your gift of this present moment.

Worry doesn't prepare you to solve problems. How can it when the problems your mind is trying to solve aren't real? And it's not protective, in fact, it's the opposite. It fills your mind with scary scenarios that grab your attention so you're less able to access your innate creativity and common sense, which we need to deal with what IS reality, which is the present moment. And it's making us very sick.

What is worry then?

It's the wisdom in our body telling us we're caught up in thought.

The reality of what eventually does happen in your life will happen as it does, and it will have nothing to do with your mind spinning stories.

What a beautiful system we have when we know it's there and we pay attention to it. Preparing can be helpful—worrying is not.

Peace of mind. It's always available to you.

And you will feel it so much more often when you step into your wisdom, and away from the busyness of your mind.

Sixty

If I haven't had a good belly laugh by lunchtime, I'm taking myself too seriously!

When was the last time you laughed out loud? And I mean not just said 'LOL', actually laughed out loud.

While many of us treat humour as a minor distraction from the 'serious business of living' it is actually an important component of a thriving life.

Apparently if you ask most people if they have a sense of humour they will say yes (as well, people universally identify themselves as being good drivers even with a stack of evidence that they're not).

How easily can you remember a joke or come up with a funny story?

Many are so unaccustomed to finding anything funny that we've lost our capacity for surprise, that is the essence of humour.

What gives humour its power in our lives is that a capacity for laughter is one of the two characteristics that separates us from other animals (the other is to contemplate our own mortality).

The best humour is in some way directed at the human condition. To be able to experience fully the sadness and suffering that life so often presents—and still find reasons to go on—is an act of courage encouraged by our ability to both love… and laugh.

To tolerate uncertainty (which is what is always forever present, and always will be, regardless of what your mind says), we must be able to cultivate daily moments of pleasure of which laughter is the ultimate.

There is so much evidence showing that humour heals. We know our health is influenced by what we think and feel about our daily lives.

Humour is also a beautiful way of connecting.

Pessimists and hypochondriacs, I guess are right in the long run. No one is getting out of here alive. But pessimism—like any attitude—is contained within a self-fulfilling prophecy. The attitude we reflect is often what we get back.

So, what makes you laugh? When was the last time you laughed?

My husband and I have some comedians we love to watch often and no matter what mood we're in or what's going on in our day, a good laugh lifts our spirits. Perhaps finding a few of those on YouTube to have on hand would be worthwhile for you too.

The seriousness of our lives and the world will still be there, but if we can find a way to laugh daily, the journey will be a bit more fun. Oh, and our health, relationships and our day might improve as well with all those feel-good chemicals. Which can only lead to more fulfilling actions.

Can you cultivate some laughter today?

Sixty One

What are the signs your self-awareness is growing?

You're starting to be able to feel your emotions as they come and go, being able to be in them without fear or reaction.

You're finding yourself becoming more accepting of your past, and noticing it shows up in your present through your mind and body reactions.

You're able to be more the observer of your thoughts, seeing them as 'not you' or 'who you are.'

You're noting the patterns of behaviour that show up repeatedly and asking yourself what you need more of with kindness instead of berating yourself.

You're observing how it's your own thinking creating your internal emotions, not anything outside of you.

You're noticing and examining your inner narrative and questioning the truth of it.

You're catching yourself more easily when you're on automatic pilot and reacting to your subconscious mind, instead of being in the flow of your day.

You're becoming more content more often with being in this present moment. 'There's nowhere you need to get to… you're already here.'

Did you notice what your mind was saying when you read these? Did it compare? Did it tell you you're not where you should be? Did it throw up that you're not getting anywhere? What did it say? You could read the above again as the observer, and the student that you are… that we all are. If you can do that, you may see where you might need a little bit more focus.

Sixty Two

Happiness is found in the small things that we often rush right past.

If there is one insight that's deepened within me during this last year, it would be this.

Life really is in the little things.

At the end of 2020 my eldest son finished his high school studies and took off to live his life. Since his departure I've found myself searching for memories of all the little things and moments with him. And sometimes I've been disheartened by the lack of memories.

Who knows why. Probably because I used to spend most of my time in my head wishing for the moment to be different. Rushing, doing, caught up in the need to be 'busy' all the time.

Or maybe I was too busy drinking alcohol or searching for that next sugary snack.

I can't get my boy back to do it all over again.

Nor can I go back and change anything. I can only

find forgiveness in myself for my choices. I did the best I could with what I knew.

I can choose at any moment to be more present and truly see the gifts that this very moment gives me.

What I see in those moments will be up to me.

Just like it will be up to you too.

Where else is life found if not in the little things?

Sixty Three

You aren't your label, you just 'think' you are.

Let's look at being insecure for example. There is no such thing as insecurity, there are only insecure thoughts.

When we start exploring who we are behind our psychology and all the labels, we often get so busy. Looking for how it should look and how it should feel. Your mind, as a part of its function, is doing its job to own this new experience, to do it for you, but it's not needed here, and you can remind it of that. Thanks, but you're not needed here.

Here's something to ponder.

What if everything you've been searching for naturally finds you when your mind falls quiet?

Minds love to generalise remember. Your brain's job is to know stuff, so it can predict stuff, so you can survive longer. It's in the survival game, not the 'peace of mind' game. Not the 'you're now good enough as you are' game. It's in many games that keep us convinced that we are something that we're not.

What could be more important for your mind to know than 'who you are'? That logical and linear machine in your head is totally invested in you having a stable and fixed personality.

Once your mind decides you're insecure for example, confirmation bias kicks in and you see proof of it everywhere.

But what about all the secure experience that moves through you as well that you miss, dismiss, or consider it a fluke? And so, insecure experience repeats itself not because it's who you are… but because you think it's who you are.

Your mind seeks to validate its experience to bolster the identity it's creating for you. It seeks to validate its experience to create a sense of safety for you (totally an illusion).

You can replace insecurity with any label you have for yourself and see this in the same way.

But the 'I am…' label is a summary of how this experience tends to show up for you. And it's an incomplete statement that is full of exceptions.

And until we see beyond all we have identified with throughout our lifetime, it will keep looking like the stuff arising in us is 'us' and 'who we are'.

It will continue to have boundaries and names that our mind recognises and labels with language. It will look solid and real and who we are. And it will continue to keep us locked in the illusion of a safe life. Wow our minds are just so busy aren't they.

But what if the traits and labels you've identified with over the years are far more in flux and far less about 'you' than they seem?

That's where we enter a whole new ball game about what's possible when it comes to living our life. When it comes to breaking free from the mental prison we innocently live in, until we see we can step free from it.

And in understanding this, we get this opportunity if we're brave enough to take it. Because we must sit in a whole lot of unknowns when we look in this direction. I think that's super cool… but I didn't in the beginning.

Your understanding of 'you' and who you are is in that beautiful little baby on the day you were born.

Everything since then has been experience, and none of it is who. you. are.

Grab that considering cup if you need to but see if you can open up yourself to consider this as possible.

Because what are your alternatives?

Sixty Four

When I took to my heart the value of kindness, it became much easier to know how to treat myself well.

For me, uncovering, owning and acting from one of my core values of kindness, truly did make it easier to treat myself well. It helped me to stop betraying myself by wanting that quick fix, that substance, or by not doing those towards moves. All because I saw deeply and honestly that all of those things weren't kindness.

When you understand the potential damage eating poorly, not moving, not sleeping well, drinking alcohol, or seeking that unearned dopamine hit does to your body, and kindness is your value, you see with clarity that continuing to act in this way goes against who you are.

Such a powerful question to ask yourself before you make a choice is, 'is this kind?' If the answer is no, then perhaps you want to really consider why you would keep doing it.

People often confuse kindness with weakness. That is a huge mistake. Kindness is strength. To choose to stay true to that value no matter what is going on in your world is the ultimate act of strength and courage. No matter what, I get to anchor what I say, what I do, and how I act to my deep core value of kindness.

As I have said previously, most of what runs our lives comes from our subconscious beliefs. And for many of us, kindness isn't one of them. Or if it is, it comes from the incorrect assumption that kindness to others helps us stay safe by being loved. If I'm kind to you, you will love me, and I will be okay. But this isn't the true essence of values. Because if it's all about what I will gain, then I'm unlikely to be able to act from this place when I'm sitting in a psychological storm.

So, while values are yours to work out for yourself—to shred the conditioned values your parents and society have given you and step into who you truly are—kindness, I believe, is a universal core one that helps us thrive.

It helps us to choose those towards moves rather than staying stuck in the damaging away ones. It helps us to anchor to strength during times of suffering. It then helps us to give this beautiful gift to others too.

And I've never met anyone who doesn't want to experience more kindness.

Sixty Five

Nothing hurts my heart more than the realisation that most people will live their entire lives never truly seeing their worth.

I want to simply pose a few questions for you to reflect on.

Do you want to spend your entire life believing you're not good enough?

Not skinny enough? Not smart enough? Not creative enough? Not… (you fill in the blanks for yourself).

I imagine the answer is no, you don't.

Then, don't just lament this; do something about it. You get to choose what you believe, and why on earth would you continue to believe you lack anything?

Do the work to see beyond the stories and connect home to yourself. Stop paying so much attention to what others and society think of you and start paying more attention to what ***you*** think of you.

When you hear your mind berating yourself, let it go.

You will have to do this hundred, maybe thousands of times.

It takes what it takes, and if you don't give up, you will eventually see those beliefs for what they are… brain junk not worthy of your attention and get on with creating a thriving life!

What are you gaining by remaining trapped in these false beliefs?

When we understand we are only ever acting from the best decision we see to make at the level of consciousness (that internal ladder) that we're sitting at, what are you gaining by not changing your choices?

It will be something.

Perhaps it's safe because no one then expects much of you. Safe because you won't fail or let yourself down. Safe because no one sees you. When you're not changing your behaviour when you know you should, there is something you are gaining from that. It's usually a made-up fear that looks like it's keeping you safe. *But is it?*

Or is it simply stopping you from living an authentic life and thriving?

That's all for today.

If you do reflect on the above questions, you will gain more clarity on what's holding you back.

And it's never anything 'out there'.

Sixty Six

We are born confident. But we're also born with an ability to convince ourselves that we're not.

Like so many of our innate gifts we are born with, over time we convince ourselves that we don't have these things and instead search outside of ourselves for the answers.

Or we convince ourselves that those gifts are only within other people.

The only time we don't feel that natural confidence, is when we're feeling self-conscious. We're focused on ourselves—what others think of us, what we know or don't know, how we look, how we sound.

That's when we're tuned in to that finite station called our mind.

But when we tune out of that and focus on the present moment and what we're trying to achieve, we will find ourselves stepping into that natural confidence that is within.

Life isn't about being like someone else.

It is about being you.

And who you are is that person when there isn't much on your mind.

When you are present to where you are right now.

Notice how you feel when you're in that place.

It's a pretty nice place to hang out, and you can go there any time you want to.

Sixty Seven

The relapse.

What gets in the way most is the fact we don't expect ourselves to experience a relapse.

We can't expect to heal years of using a substance like sugar and alcohol without ever using it again.

I don't like the word relapse or setback.

Because it comes with judgements, timelines, and stigma. None of which is particularly helpful when we're on the healing road. But all things our mind just loves to offer up.

But we cannot ignore the fact that the sugar or alcohol (or whatever it may be for you) monster may rise, more than a few times, on its journey to a final demise.

Just know, that even with the best of intentions and the strongest of commitments, you may, at some point, allow your drug back into your life.

And the more you can face this reality rather than running from it, the more you will use it for what it is… a teaching experience.

But these experiences are usually incredibly painful. I promise you; I know this.

The gremlins seem to awaken stronger than ever. You find yourself spiralling down to the weeds so quickly you appear lost to its power.

You may lose trust in your own judgement, resolve and strength. You may find yourself self-loathing, full of shame and in despair. So deep again it seems like healing isn't possible.

But recovering from substance abuse is a war, with the highest stakes imaginable. For me, the most terrifying thing when I relapsed was how easy it was to believe that, because of the relapse, I had lost the war. Society tells us if we're unable to stick to our decisions, we're weak. If we break promises, we can't be trusted. It's so easy to believe that making mistakes makes us useless. We figure if we 'fall off that wagon' we may as well 'go all the way' because it's 'too late now.'

We feel beyond repair, no longer worth fixing. We pile up internal guilt, convinced we deserve the hatred of those we love. So, we punish ourselves with more of our drug in a bid to numb ourselves from all the horror.

I have been there.

But it is a mistake to believe that by losing a battle, we have lost the war.

The truth is that each battle makes us stronger as long as we remain committed to a better tomorrow. We must fight this battle with compassion and forgiveness.

We must allow that lost battle to be a reminder of all the reasons we wanted to quit rather than an unforgivable mistake.

The relapse experience will remind you of why you stopped. Your body will hurt, your mind will be foggy, your guts will complain, and if it's drinking—you will remember how it felt to nurse a hangover. You will remember the internal struggles, the recrimination, the deception.

Let these experiences tell you a story of how far you've come. Let them be what they are, a steppingstone on your journey.

Sometimes we forget why we started on the path. The pain of using fades and we wonder if we can moderate it. Our mind offers up the idea that maybe we can. Maybe we're missing out. Maybe we're feeling isolated and disconnected. You wonder whether using again will bring you back these connections and fill that void the substance used to fill for you.

But a substance can never heal these things.

And it's very hard to do this on your own, even though you may want to hide because of the shame.

You can overcome this.

Let each temptation, each battle bring you closer to winning the war. Learn from each experience. Discover the truth about your drug and its role in your life.

Sugar. Carbs. Alcohol. It doesn't define you.

It does not give you your worth.

It is not who you are.

It will not fix your problems, solve your loneliness, or provide you with any answers that you seek. It will not make you more accepted.

This is a journey. Not a destination. It is a road that no one else can walk but you. These are choices that no one can make but you.

But know that by committing to a different future, no matter how many battles you have ahead of you, the war has already been won.

Sixty Eight

Don't be so busy proving your worth that you forget to be true to yourself.

Is there a small voice within you calling you home? We all have it, but often it's drowned out by the outside noise, and the conditioned stories our mind and nervous system.

This voice has an important message for you and if you can lean in and listen, you will hear.

It's asking for truth.

It's asking for presence.

It's asking for alignment between who you are at your core, and how you present to the world.

We can set off on a discovery and follow it home and put down anchor in what is real, being ourselves. Or we can spend our life adrift with our worth sitting in what isn't real… in other's reactions, opinions, and the stories we've built inside to stay safe.

But to find all that we seek, we must remember our core values. If we don't know what these are for ourselves, we don't have boundaries… we have reactions.

Sixty Nine

'Do you love Me?' Alice asked.

'No, I don't love you!' replied the White Rabbit.

Alice frowned and clasped her hands together as she did whenever she felt hurt.

'See?' replied the White Rabbit. 'Now you're going to start asking yourself what makes you so imperfect and what did you do wrong so that I can't love you at least a little.

You know, that's why I can't love you. You will not always be loved Alice, there will be days when others will be tired and bored with life, will have their heads in the clouds, and will hurt you.

Because people are like that, they somehow always end up hurting each other's feelings, whether through carelessness, misunderstanding, or conflicts with themselves.

If you don't love yourself, at least a little, if you don't create an armour of self-love and happiness around your heart, the feeble annoyances caused by others will become lethal and will destroy you.

The first time I saw you I made a pact with myself: 'I will avoid loving you until you learn to love yourself'.'

Lewis Carrol, *Alice in Wonderland*

Seventy

The path of healing is not a straight line. It's a spiral. We return time and again to the lessons we need to see.

Can you look back and see how far you've travelled?

The journey towards fully loving yourself as you are, is always full of stops, starts, backward steps, detours.

There will be many times that you will doubt yourself.

Doubt you have even progressed.

Doubt you even have the potential to change.

But you can, you have, and you will.

You know you simply could not have gotten to where you are today without every single movement and pause you ever made.

Embrace it all.

Seventy One

You are not broken, and you never have been.

When you feel that you are, it's just that you have innocently lost sight of the gifts that naturally live within you.

A big part of my coaching is showing my clients that they have innate gifts, like confidence, resilience, love, compassion, joy, peace, optimism and more within them, but that they also have the capacity to convince themselves that they don't have them.

How could healing and change look differently to you if you see you're not fixing anything because nothing is broken?

Instead, all you need to do is reconnect with the innate abilities that live within you and live your life in the way you want to live it.

I spent my life with no idea that I had access to these things within me.

I thought I had to find them from out there somewhere.

I thought many times I was broken.

But I just didn't know what to do about it other than just keep 'working on myself'.

I thought everyone else just had it, and I didn't.

Especially when it came to motivation or self-discipline.

Nope, I thought. Everyone else has it all together except for me.

It's a very typical characteristic of someone who doesn't know about their own innate gifts.

They think they're on their own, that they are the only one.

But you never are.

Now I know what's hidden within us all, I just love showing others how to tune in and reconnect with their innate wellbeing too.

Imagine if you didn't have to search any longer?

What if you're already home?

How would that change your life?

Seventy Two

You are exactly where you are meant to be. You're not behind in life. How can you be?

Can you pause and consider this for a minute.

Resist doing what your brain loves to do, which is to instantly dismiss new information that doesn't align with its current beliefs.

Instead, just put it 'over there' for a while and ponder this.

What if it were true?

What if you are exactly where you're meant to be?

You see… you are.

And accepting this brings freedom and growth.

Resistance to this brings suffering and a feeling of 'stuck-ness.'

Every decision you've ever made in your life up to this point has been because it was the best decision you saw to do in that moment.

Every time.

While we may ‘know’ that it’s not the ‘best’ decision to make for the longer term, in that moment it is the best we see to do with the level of awareness we have.

And awareness is infinite.

When we see more, we can do more.

In fact, we all have access to a penthouse of awareness above us, even if we only ever feel like we’re in the basement.

Just knowing the possibilities awareness brings can open our eyes to see more.

We only need to make a choice to do so.

If you can free yourself from your past and accept where you are today, your world will open.

Look up.

What do you see?

What is good about where you are today?

Can you even go back to change the past?

So, what would be the point in letting it dictate what you see in this present moment or any future ones?

You only have now.

Seventy Three

How can you get better at something that you keep avoiding? If you wanted to learn to play the piano, and never sat down and practiced, you would never improve. Eating well is the same. You can't master what you avoid.

What's on your plate today?

Is it going to nourish your mind, body and soul?

It's a simple question, and well worth asking yourself every single day.

Your body deserves to feel good.

It can only feel good if you feed it well.

So feed it well.

Seventy Four

Where are you today, head or heart?

I simply love this insight from one of my beautiful clients.

Did you know you have a choice as to what drives your day?

But if we don't pause to make a conscious decision, then we will be driven around by our habitual mind, totally missing most of what goes on in your day.

The heart always knows.

It whispers kindly, and you can only hear it when you stop listening to your loud habitual mind.

So where are you today, head or heart?

Another great question to ask yourself at the beginning of every day.

Seventy Five

Boundaries are the direct expression of our core values. If we don't know what our core values are, we don't have boundaries. We have reactions.

I've been having some wonderfully insightful discussions about boundaries with the coaches I'm currently mentoring within The Thriving Place.

It can take tremendous courage to set boundaries in your work and life if you're used to being a people pleaser, and you've innocently tied your self-worth to how others feel about you.

I used to be terrified of disappointing others by setting boundaries.

In fact, for most of my life I'm not sure I even knew what they were.

I had so many protective layers on me that said things like, if I disappointed others then they wouldn't love me and my whole internal world would crash.

Slowly, one by one I removed those many layers and insightfully started to see that even if I disappointed others, I was ok. Especially if I was being true to myself and protecting my core value.

I saw that setting boundaries and respecting them within myself was an act of self-love.

And I also saw it was an act of love to others around me if I freed them to do the same.

If you have trouble setting boundaries with others, or respecting their boundary setting, there's so much you can do to grow in that area.

It is very uncomfortable at first, but we don't need to fear discomfort.

Indeed, it is our bodies way of telling us we're growing.

We're transforming.

Wellbeing lives within you.

Nothing, or no one can take that away from you.

Knowing the capital 'T' truth in that makes it easier to step out into the unknown, because we all have access to a universal safety net whether we know it or not.

We are always protected.

Only you know if this is an area within you that requires more of your internal focus.

Don't fear looking within.

It's where the magic lives.

Seventy Six

Not every weight is worth carrying. Let it go.

What mental baggage could you release that could change your life?

The expectations you have on yourself.

The stories you keep hearing within yourself and believing.

The perceived expectations you feel others have placed on you.

Most of us are walking around carrying a huge amount of mental weight which can make travelling through life hard work and exhausting.

Did you know you can let go of anything you want to?

Every single one of them.

But there is a catch.

You must make that choice to do so, which requires you to be brave and vulnerable.

Being brave and vulnerable are two things that can look super scary when we don't know that we have a universal safety net protecting us. Always.

Do you want to carry all this extra weight around with you for the rest of your life?

I didn't.

You can let it go.

Seventy Seven

You are more changeable than you think.

What two things do you need to know this more deeply?

You must want it.

Sounds obvious but so much of what we try to do we don't really want.

Find a way to want it, and it will become much easier.

Don't fear the awakening.

Accept it will look different.

Be ok with that.

Be ok with not knowing how it will evolve.

Embrace the journey.

If not now, when?

Seventy Eight

What is stopping you from moving towards your health goals?

More often than not, in my work I see overwhelmingly it comes down to one of two things.

One is when we 'think' we already know what we need to do.

Thinking we already know closes us off to learning or seeing anything new. So, we just keep doing what we 'know' over and over even when it's clearly not working.

The thing is, we can never know everything on any subject and accepting that will naturally open us up to wanting to see something new.

The second one is we are afraid.

We fear what we might see, we fear not knowing, we fear failing, we fear the changes we might have to make, we fear the discomfort.

It all just looks like a huge pit of fear that in the end

keeps us from taking even one small step.

The good news is this type of fear lessons with understanding.

Over our lifetime we do create beliefs, stories and patterns that look a whole lot like truth. Truth about who we are, what we can do, what we can achieve, and what it all means.

There is nothing I love more than disrupting this thinking and showing how it's possible to not buy in to any of it. It's all an illusion and like any illusion, it's not real, no matter how good the illusionist is.

And if it's not real we don't have to pay attention to any of it!

I used to 'argue for my limitations'.

I used to tell myself that I couldn't do this or that, I wasn't that sort of person, I had to be this or that.

I argued for my limitations and guess what?

That's what I got. Limits!

So, what is holding you back?

The good news is you don't even have to articulate what it is.

You just need to see that nothing can hold you back, except what you think.

Seventy Nine

I am so tired of starting things and failing.

The lament of almost every single client when they begin working with me.

It's not your fault, and you haven't failed.

You've just been innocently looking in the wrong direction for change.

When you shift your focus and look down a totally different path, change becomes effortless.

The first step is acceptance.

You can't change the past and it doesn't have to define your present or future.

The second step is to know that it is your attention to your thoughts that dictate your behaviour in every minute of every day.

And it is totally optional which thoughts you want to grab hold of.

It really is.

Your brain hates change, and it will do anything it can to stop you.

But with the benefit of insight, you can overcome all of that and find the freedom to flow effortlessly through life.

All you must do, is to want it.

Then choose it.

Then do it.

Eighty

What is something that simply can't be avoided if we want to change?

Discomfort.

If you have created a habit that you no longer want to do because it is not serving you, there is no way you can change this without sitting through some discomfort.

The key is that we don't have to fear that.

We're born to handle discomfort.

Our mind loves to scream at us that we're not, but that's not worth your attention remember.

Many of my clients want to end a lifetime of emotional eating, boredom eating, emotional drinking.

Expecting this process to be both quick and painless is setting you up to fail.

It won't be quick, and it won't be painless.

Every time the urge hits to repeat your habit, you

need to ride through it. If you obey the urge, you strengthen it. Every time you let it pass, it weakens.

The power moves from the habitual brain, back to you.

Focus on each day and do this each time when your urge hits, and over time you will become free. Your urge won't have any hold over you. It won't feel uncomfortable, it won't feel compelling. It won't scare you.

It will be easy for you to dismiss it.

But you can't get to that magical place without going through the uncomfortable experience.

Imagine a day when you will be free from your habit?

The power is within you, and this is in your hands.

Eighty One

Certainty is never taking a risk. You're certain to never get what you want if you don't even try.

I took my son to the basketball courts today. It made me think of this truth.

If we never even give it go, well of course nothing will change.

I've been having lots of conversations with my boys today around changing the words

'I can't'

to

'I've never learnt.'

So many times, we tell ourselves—and believe it—that we can't do something.

But we've just never learnt.

We can learn anything; we just have to do the work to learn it.

What if you get curious about what you believe you can’t do?

I bet if you’re honest with yourself, you will acknowledge that you’ve just never learnt.

And if you’re still here, you’ve got time!

Eighty Two

An old Cherokee told his grandson,
'My son, there is a battle between two wolves inside us all. One is evil. It is anger, jealousy, greed, resentment, inferiority, lies and ego. The other is good. It is joy, peace, love, hope, humility, kindness, empathy and truth.' The boy thought about it, and asked, 'Grandfather, which wolf wins?' The old man quietly replied, 'The one you feed.'
Author unknown

I first heard this story from one of my teachers. It is a story that reflects the capacity inside of humans.

When we're unconscious and lack awareness, we are at the mercy of the evil wolf. Everyone is 'just in our way' and we are centred on that one person that sits at the centre of our universe, ourselves. We're in the rat race, we are operating in some default setting, but we feel a constant gnawing sense of having had, and lost, some infinite thing.

The alternative is consciousness. Awareness. Choice.

Deciding how to think about any and every situation

you're confronted with.

Deciding not to judge, not to assume or think you know about everyone and everything.

What's most important about all of this is that you get to decide.

Which one will you feed?

Eighty Three

What opens your heart up to gratitude? Do more of that.

I have a few daily practices that help me to remember what I'm grateful for. They come naturally with the rising and setting of the sun. Sunlight is a healer, and getting out in the light every day is a part of keeping your mind and body working optimally. Because of this, it also feels good, so it naturally opens yourself up to noticing more of what is good in your life.

At the start of each day, I cultivate my conscious mind. What does that mean? It means I get present, I remember my core values, and I remember that I get to choose how I react to what happens in my day. I don't get to choose what happens, but how I react to what happens is up to me.

I greet the day with love and gratitude, both for it, and for myself. I am here, which means I have opportunities.

Yesterday has gone, tomorrow hasn't come. Today is all I have.

How will I choose to be in it?

What loving choices can I choose towards myself and others?

At the end of each day, I reflect.

What loving choices (towards moves) did I make for me today?

Breathe them in.

Don't rush off!

Where did I make a choice out of habit, from my past, that looked loving in the moment, but wasn't? What can I learn from that?

What can I see I could do differently next time?

What core value didn't I remember?

Every day is a gift.

Do you choose to open it?

Eighty Four

To love oneself is the beginning of a life-long romance.
Oscar Wilde

How long has it been since you've caught a glimpse of your authentic self?

Smiling, positive, upbeat, calm, reassuring, confident.

Look in the mirror. Can you see this person?

She/he is in there, and part of your transformation is reconnecting back with her/him.

If you get quiet and spend some time reflecting, I just know you will be able to recall a time (hopefully many) when you felt in the flow of your life.

Things just went right; everything fell into place.

And in this place, is where our true authentic self lives.

This is our natural state. It is our birth right to feel like this.

And when you don't feel like this, where is your mind?

Focused on all those stories and thoughts that seem like they just go round and round like a treadmill getting you nowhere fast and leaving you feeling constantly exhausted.

Your authentic self doesn't live here.

So how do we tap into this natural state more often?

Firstly, we need to know it exists and we need to believe it's possible.

And then it will grow and grow.

Then we need to tune in to it.

Switch the stations over and tune in more to the feelings within your body.

Do what feels good.

Be present in the moment.

Tune in to feelings within your body.

Most importantly, be open to change.

Welcome it.

Don't go unconscious, be awake.

Think, grow, find joy, pause, slow down.

When you can do that, you will hear.

Your authentic self has been speaking to you all along.

It's time you tuned in and listened.

Eighty Five

The change journey might last for the rest of your life. Isn't that amazing to think all you can learn about yourself, and your body is infinite?

As a metabolic health and life coach my job is to help people successfully regain their health and life through a combination of lifestyle changes and understanding what it takes to make real and sustainable change.

The magical formula of healing mind and body.

I don't work with anyone who still wants the quick fix or short-term diet plan.

However, even though many of my clients say they don't want that anymore, they do have a whole lot of habitual thinking around how eating should be controlled, restricted, and look a certain way, and they innocently are controlled by all those stories until I show them the illusion that these are.

There's nothing wrong with wanting to lose weight.

But the problem is that we, as a society and then individually equate weight loss with health.

However, they're not necessarily the same thing.

I can help anyone lose weight. You can do it eating just potatoes, as has been shown. If you restrict your calories, you will lose weight.

That is, until your metabolism and hormones are so damaged that strategy just won't work anymore.

The reality of this that is difficult for people to acknowledge is that you're not gaining health eating food this way.

If you're not eating a nutrient dense diet, your body will be getting what it needs from somewhere else. This often looks like the breakdown of your own muscle and bone.

That is, until it can't do that anymore, and you risk sarcopenia, osteoporosis, and the like.

If you come to the low carb/keto/carnivore lifestyle prepared to do the work to make it a lifestyle, it will be the last 'diet' you will ever do.

How would that feel for you?

The hard part is though, you must be in for the long game!

Learn to step away from your habitual mind that tells you that you want it now. That it must be fixed overnight. That you must be perfect, that you must get it right from the start. Tells you can you start Monday, to have something once because you've been good all day, to eat the whole packet because you've had one, that you can't change, that you are not disciplined, that you can't do it… blah blah blah blah!!!

That is unhelpful self-talk and all it does is keep you doing the same things over and over and is simply not worthy of your attention, let alone doing as it commands.

Metabolic health is your birthright. I will say that again.

Metabolic health is your birthright!

And if we were living in an environment that promoted health instead of profits, it would be a lot easier.

But we don't live in that environment.

And while people like the 2020 Australian of the Year, Dr James Muecke and others are trying to change this, you are not powerless to be able to do this yourself.

You can get to a point where you are not influenced by the outside world, by what your family eat, by what your friends eat.

You can sit with joy in doing what works for you, and release everyone around you to do what works for them.

But you need to take responsibility for your own life to do this. And if you're used to giving this away to others, this can feel mighty uncomfortable at first.

With the right support, you can absolutely do this and free yourself from the habitual dieting cycle once and for all.

Change isn't usually about doing the same things harder.

It's about doing a complete U-turn and heading down a totally different path.

Eighty Six

You are imperfectly perfect, just as you are.

You really are.

I have a lot of conversations around this ‘myth’ of perfection.

The idea that a ‘perfect’ exists, holds people back from the actual doing.

It’s so easy to fall for the story that says, if it’s not perfection, it’s not worth doing.

But when we start to unpack what ‘perfection’ really is, we can start to see through it.

‘Perfection’ is a bar we internally create.

It’s self-imposed, and when we don’t reach it, we berate ourselves and think it means something about our worth.

It does not.

And while it’s a strong story, it is all an illusion.

If we can poke holes through it and stop being taken in by it, we will start to free ourselves from its grips.

And instead, we can simply show up to life, do our best from our heart, accept the outcome

… and know it was good enough.

Eighty Seven

I'm learning to hold my beliefs lightly. Can you?

Let's look at why this is such a beautiful concept to embrace.

Over our lifetime we develop beliefs based on our experiences, interactions, and conditioning.

Every human being on the planet has a unique belief system, which means it would be impossible for us to see anything in the same way someone else does… or for others to see things as we do. This is not the first time I have said this in this book.

When you understand this deeply there is no logical reason to take personally what other people say and do.

Your mind interprets circumstances in your day in the context of what it already knows and believes to be true.

And because your beliefs are unique to you, the interpretation of any situation will vary accordingly, from person to person.

If we understand and accept this, this difference can be a source of wisdom, joy, and humour, instead of frustration and judgement.

Essentially, if our experiences, interactions, and conditioning had been different, our beliefs and interpretations would be different.

Did you also know that we all have a vested interest in validating our own set of beliefs? They don't like to be threatened or tampered with. Notice what your mind does when you come across someone who doesn't believe what you do? See how it looks to invalidate what the other person is saying, all the way down to making it personal about the person saying it.

When you come armed with a deep knowing of how this all works and come up against someone who sees the situation differently to you (especially someone you love), you can instead approach with a genuine interest in and a respect for their view in life.

If you can do that, defences drop… and hearts open.

And when that happens, you have a far greater chance at having much more fulfilling relationships and connections, even with people you never thought possible.

Wouldn't that create a more peaceful feeling in your world?

Eighty Eight

Where is your focus today?

There is so much wisdom to be found in the present moment.

It's all we ever have, yet often we live way more in our minds, either thinking about the past or some imagined future.

What we don't realise when that happens, is that we're limiting our ability to deal with what is right in front of us today.

We often spend so much time in our heads, that we're left exhausted and don't have a lot of resources to deal with reality.

Who exactly are we having a conversation with?

It's so easy to just blindly follow our habitual mind.

But there's not much wisdom to be found there, and usually it keeps us in the same places that just aren't serving us.

And it's exhausting.

But there is another way.

Notice the feeling you're sitting in.

Does it feel good or not so good?

The feeling we sit in is a guide to where our focus is. When we're in our head, we feel it in our body. Our body is a great mirror of our mind. When it's calm, our body feels calm. When it's all sped up and full of thinking, we feel like that in our body as well.

I often tell my clients to follow the feeling. It never lets us down and is our wisdom reminding us to slow down and focus our attention back on the present moment… which is all we have.

Our thinking is untrustworthy. Most of what it tells us is habitual stories that just serve to keep us from seeing the magic in the now.

You know that's happening when you don't feel good.

I rarely trust my thinking now. Especially thinking that tells me, 'I can't', 'I'm not good enough', 'I'm not as good as her', 'you must eat that food to feel better'.

All these stories are so limiting. The illusion of safety is so real, but it's simply that… an illusion.

So where is your focus today?

Start creating the habit of awareness.

That's all you need to start to do to create a shift from

within you.

Are you in your head or in your life?

Eighty Nine

The day you decide to stop running away from yourself is the day your life will change.

Over the years, my work has taken me into mentoring other coaches. This has evolved as people have reached out to me to ask for help in either getting started as a coach, or to learn how to help people with real, sustained, change.

I really enjoy it, and realised this is the area I want to do more work in.

Authenticity is a word that is thrown around a lot, yet I don't see a lot of it really.

I see a lot of people pretending, faking it till they make it, or looking to emulate what other people are doing/have done. Performing, being what people think they should be, wearing masks.

The thing is, everyone can be authentic, but they're often innocently searching in the wrong place to find it.

True authenticity comes from within, which comes from looking within.

Looking at our triggers, our behaviour, our feelings for messages and wisdom, and decided not to run from them anymore.

Not looking outside to numb, forget, relieve.

Not blaming anyone else for what is inherently ours.

And watching the natural transformation that comes from that.

For these are our greatest teachers.

And that is what builds an authentic coach.

The day you decide to stop running away from yourself is the day your life will change.

And so how will you show up to every day precious day to impact everyone else around you?

Ninety

Are you driven to eat when you don't feel good?

I ate when I felt stressed, sad, or upset for 35 years.

I hated being driven by something that didn't feel like me.

But I didn't feel like I had a choice but to search for that relief.

Until one day I saw that I did.

I saw it wasn't my fault I did it. I saw I wasn't broken or defective.

Rather, I was innocently acting out of a misguided sense of self love. I was driven to make myself feel better, even though I knew it wasn't good for me.

It was all an innocent misunderstanding.

I was shown that I didn't have to fear my emotions. I didn't have to follow my habitual brain to do what it was telling me to do.

With time, compassion, and love for myself, I saw

that I could sit in an uncomfortable feeling, which was sometimes unbearable, but I was still okay.

I saw it pass; I didn't have to act.

I really was ok.

I was shown to look within.

I was made aware that my discomfort was coming from my own thinking, and I didn't have to fear my own thinking.

I was shown it was my brain doing what brains do.

But I had the benefit of insight and wisdom that could take me beyond those unhelpful habitual patterns.

Now I am free from the grips of eating when I'm not feeling good.

I eat what I want, when I want, without doing it from a place of discomfort or searching for relief.

I still have urges sometimes, but that's okay.

I don't have to fear them. It's my relationship to them that matters, and I can choose to follow that thinking or not.

Woohoo! I am a normal human being, just like you.

I have experienced so much freedom from this inside out understanding.

I hope I am showing you the freedom that is available for you too… if you look within to find it.

Ninety One

I can now see that sitting in an uncomfortable feeling is going to lead to growth.

One of my clients said this in a session when we were talking about the discomfort that naturally comes with change.

Such beautiful wisdom, that it bought tears to my eyes.

Because it is true. Discomfort is a normal part of growth. The less we fear it and embrace it as a natural and normal part of evolving as a human being, the more insight we will come out the other side with.

And it is this insight that naturally leads to change.

Insight. From within.

A shifting of the beliefs and thoughts to allow space for new ideas, fresh thoughts that lead to new behaviours.

Ninety Two

If we keep striving for perfection, we need to examine the trauma that told us perfection is the only way we can be loved.

Oh, how much I've seen about the 'myth of perfection' in recent years.

I don't think there was a specific moment when I decided that perfection didn't exist, and that any ideas I had about what it might have meant was completely made up.

It was more like a slow evolution.

Little by little, insight by insight, I saw that when I was able to drop the stories I had in my head about who I had to be, what I had to achieve, how I had to behave, the kind of mum, wife, friend, coach I thought I had to be, I was able to create space for who I really was to shine through.

What I hadn't realised, was these stories were creating the false belief that who I was, wasn't enough.

That it was never enough because there was always

something more that I had to do.

But the thing is… we are enough.

We were born enough!

I had just convinced myself through these stories that the opposite was true.

You see, when we focus on the stories, we don't hear our wisdom gently guiding us, nudging us, and protecting us while we show up and just be as we are in the world in all our glory. Our design is amazing and our connection with life has our back.

Doing what we do in the world from a place of 'lack' and the myth of being less than perfect or doing what we do in the world from a place of abundance and being 'already there'?

I know what looks a whole lot more fun to me!

Ninety Three

You really are naturally confident. What would you change in your life if you started to believe in this truth?

I promise you this is true. It's only your mind you need to convince.

I received this message from a beautiful friend who was about to step totally out of her comfort zone to do some public speaking.

This was her message:

'Hi Tracey,

I have a little bit of news to tell you…

I'm terrified… but I have been asked to give a speech.

If you can give me some of your magic…

I'd be eternally grateful!

I'm not practiced in public speaking!'

We feel a ‘lack’ of confidence when we’re focused on ourselves. We feel self-conscious.

Don’t grab those thoughts!

Think about the audience and how much they want to hear your message.

Connect with them, think about why they’re here with you, and let your natural, beautiful self-shine.’

She nailed it of course.

It’s all about shifting your awareness.

That’s where the answers to growth are found.

Ninety Four

To make a different choice feels like work. Don't let that stop you.

You do get to choose whether you will be led by your sub-conscious mind to make your decisions every day or decide to make a different choice.

If you don't decide to choose differently, you simply won't.

It can be as simple as waking up each day and consciously deciding to choose nutrient dense foods for that day.

Then to keep choosing to follow that conscious thinking and let all the other thinking pass without giving it your attention.

Then every morning waking up and making a conscious choice again, to choose health.

Just for that day.

Imagine where you would be in a year from now if you did that every day?

Simple, yet not easy and most definitely uncomfortable.

But growth lives in the discomfort, and we can learn to love that place for what it brings us.

Ninety Five

How to comfort yourself without food.

We've all learned coping behaviours that align with food. We learned to eat when we were sad, hurt, bored or in any way uncomfortable. Over time, this became the subconscious response when we were sitting in an uncomfortable emotion, which we must start to notice to challenge it.

Relearning new ways to comfort yourself when you feel pushed around by your moods and emotions is an essential part of healing.

Learning new ways to comfort yourself dramatically increases self-trust. It also lets you know that whatever arises, you can deal with it.

But you can't deal with anything you keep running away from or you can't even see.

New self-soothing skills can be easily learned, but like anything new, they must be practised. And of course, you will be coming up against your mighty subconscious mind, so it will require you to become present and conscious.

When you learn these new skills, you will be helping to build a resilient nervous system. You will help your body to switch off the fight/fight/freeze response that creates all the discomfort within your body.

It will bring you to an increased level of awareness and help you in your quest to be a witness to your thoughts, thus coping with it all far more effectively (and no need to reach for the food).

Trust yourself that switching to soothe is possible. Here’s how.

Recognise the symptoms of panic, anxiety, or mounting fear. You will feel them in your body as I’ve said repeatedly. Know you’re capable of switching to soothe. Become aware of what your subconscious mind wants you to do (hint: it will be a very familiar pattern to you when you look).

Tell yourself as often as you can, ‘I CAN deal with this.’ This powerful message will affect you physically and emotionally. It doesn’t matter that you don’t know how to deal with it; what matters is that you will.

While you’re telling yourself ‘I can deal with this,’ you are not able to stay in that loop of how awful it is, how hopeless you are, how frightful and disappointing life is.

Write down what the issue is (another gold for your journal). Putting it ‘out there’ on a piece of paper makes space in your mind. It also gives you a little distance. Use as few words as possible to describe it.

Ask yourself, ‘Does this need my attention now?’

Often when we're in a panic, you are the least creative or effective. If the matter isn't urgent, switch your attention to something else, like your doorway to peace.

Your mind can only think about one thing at a time. Switch your mind from victim to problem solver. Sit up straight, breathe deeply, shoulders back. Your mind will immediately benefit.

Learn not to trust your decision making in these times. Your thinking will be distorted and so will your reactions. Take your time. Focus on calming yourself first, and only then on dealing with the issue or problem.

Sometimes you need to get some physical distance from what's worrying you. You won't take the problem with you if you tell yourself that you're in the process of dealing with it.

Do something that is physically demanding. Digging your garden, walking briskly, swimming… what the activity is will be less important than acting, changing your environment, and with that, your thoughts, and feelings.

If your mind keeps taking you back (I'm sure it will) to the issue, just repeat the same steps. 'I can deal with this'; writing down the problem; switching your attention; doing something physically demanding. Also remind yourself that clarity isn't found in the weeds. It comes when it clears. Get bored with this process. It will help you.

When things have cleared up and you're feeling calmer, look at what you've written down. Do you see the problem or issue differently now? If so, write down what you see.

Now ask yourself, who is the wisest, cleverest, and kindest person I know? (You don't have to know them personally). Once you have identified this person, ask yourself. 'How would they deal with this?'

Do not underestimate the power of your own imagination. It is your thoughts themselves that have produced those powerful systems of stress or anxiety. Harness that same imaginative power now to support you and see what needs to be done—if anything.

Write down what you imagine their answer would be. The insights you are looking for will be helpful, kind, supportive and manageable.

Know that some problems are not going to be solved; they will only be outlived. Recognising the truth of that can also be surprisingly soothing.

Notice as often as you can just how severe a problem looks and feels when you are hungry, exhausted, overwhelmed or stressed.

It's the perfect storm for your subconscious mind to take over. Use your panic as the wisdom it is—an invaluable alarm bell on your dashboard wanting you to pay more attention to your life.

Ask yourself: what extra stress is happening right now in my life? What would help me deal with this stress?

Who could I talk to about this?

How have I got through this kind of tough time before?

Remind yourself that whatever is happening is not all of who you are; nor is it how things will always be.

You can deal with this.

Ninety Six

Free yourself to focus on the process rather than your fears.

There is real freedom in shifting your focus from your fears to the process.

Our culture is highly critical and super competitive.

It's almost impossible for this not to influence your attitudes and judgements.

But what joy to know you can do well in your life without judging yourself through the eyes of other people or constantly comparing yourself to them.

It has been very well shown in the world of psychology that if you resist the competitiveness of our culture and just focus on the task at hand for yourself, you will do better at whatever you are tackling.

You stop constantly assessing your performance, worrying about it and comparing because you're absorbed by what you're doing… you are present and giving it your full attention.

You may still come out on top at times.

But that is a distant second place to the deep satisfaction that comes with feeling better about yourself and what you're doing.

And the flow-on effect from this is pretty impressive.

You get more done.

You can afford to be encouraging of others, not critical.

You can be generous instead of cynical or envious.

Your idea of success expands.

People are friends, not competitors.

You don't live in fear of 'failing'.

Your innate abilities bubble to the surface and flourish.

How good does that sound?

Ninety Seven

Being 'ready' isn't a real concept. It's one we think we will feel when the time is right. But that's not how our mind works. It is designed to keep you safe, not get you 'ready' for growth.

Minds are goals shifters.

It constantly suggests you put off action because action is risky. When you know this, you can learn to step over it. To step forward into creation and action, even if you don't 'feel' ready.

Feelings shift with action.

You learn.

You grow.

You experience richness.

You make mistakes.

You learn.

Sitting in the waiting room may be safe, but life slips away that place.

You can start creating no matter where you are right now. And grow as you go.

We are all getting older, and time stands still for no one. We have no choice in that.

But we do get to choose how we live.

How are you choosing to live?

Ninety Eight

It is the direction that matters most. And that direction is within.

Time is not what heals.

You are the key to your own healing, and it comes from the journey within.

Without doing this, hurt, trauma and deep conditioning will continue to sit in your thoughts, impacting your behaviour.

What ultimately heals is self-love.

Going in to let go.

Going in to see you are everything you have been searching for.

This is your birthright.

It is all yours for the taking if you choose it.

Ninety Nine

Your beliefs act like filters on a camera changing how you see the world. And your biology adapts to those beliefs. When we truly recognise that our beliefs are that powerful, we hold the key to freedom.

Dr Bruce Lipton

Do you believe in yourself? Do you believe you can be well? Do you believe life is loving? Do you believe humans are love at their essence?

Whatever you believe, is what you will see. And when it comes to healing, being healthy, and getting your body to function metabolically well, you must believe it is possible. You must believe you can do what is necessary for you to achieve it.

Because if you don't… you won't.

The body follows the mind. So, where you want to go, you must create the mind conditions to take you there. I've shown you many ways to do that within the pages of this book. But a great place to start is in becoming more conscious and aware of that choice point before action.

What most people don't realise is that our subconscious patterns largely drive us. And these don't stand a chance against positive thinking or affirmations. You have to go deeper than that. You need to look at what those beliefs, patterns, and safety responses that routinely run your behaviour and ask whether they align with your core values, and your desires, dreams, and wishes for the life you want to create.

The most common subconscious belief that runs people's lives centres around worth. That you're not worth it, that who you are—as you are—isn't enough, that you don't deserve to be healthy, well, and vibrant.

You will know if this is a belief of yours, because you will sabotage yourself often. You will treat yourself in a way that is misaligned with what you want. You will say things like, 'I know what to do, but…'

Your heart may want health, but if your subconscious belief is that you don't deserve it you will be locked in a battle that could last for the rest of your life.

The good news is that you can change this.

How?

The subconscious can only be changed through action. Your actions can either reflect lack or love. Your actions can either reflect love or fear. There is no grey in this.

Take a look at the actions you take each day. Do they reflect a deep love and a belief in yourself, or the opposite? Be honest. It's the only way you can truly turn the ship around.

To change the deep belief that you are indeed worth

it as you are, you need to start acting like it. Whether you feel like it or not. You need to bring in the free will that comes when we turn on the power of our conscious mind and decide that your worth came with you at birth. You deserve to walk this earth in your full capacity that is loving, kind, and worthy.

Then when you are at that magical choice point before you take action, you need to ask yourself the question.

'Am I acting from my old subconscious beliefs, or from who I know I am. From love?'

Let that be your anchor. Let that guide you. Make that affirmation a living and breathing truth by seeing it being reflected in your day-to-day actions.

Treat yourself with love and kindness every single day you're alive. Kindness isn't giving yourself what you think you want in this moment. It's giving yourself what you know in your heart you need and deserve for now, and for the future you are wanting.

Decide to do this daily. And over time, those deep-seated beliefs of your worth will change. Especially when it comes to healing. In order to achieve it, you must believe. Believe you can. Believe you deserve it. Then let all the other mind junk flow right on by.

Spend some time reflecting on your deep beliefs. You may not be able to consciously articulate them, but if you have the courage to look at your daily behaviour towards yourself and others, you will see what your subconscious believes.

One Hundred

You are not lost. You never have been. This journey home to yourself is a great remembering.

Are you ready for the magical inward journey?

Are you ready to step into the life you deserve to live?

Are you ready to see that you are everything you've been searching for?

Pick up your perfectly imperfect self and off you go.

Take me with you. I will walk beside you the entire time.

If you fall, brush yourself off and get back up.

It never matters how fast you travel, only that you do.

Forgive yourself quickly, forgive others too.

If you forget, like we all do, that's okay.

Gently remind yourself of your humanness and get

back on the path.

You only have this one beautiful life.

Embrace it all.

The End…

Or, I deeply hope for you, it has been a new beginning.

Books Mentioned

Brukner, Peter Dr. (2018). *A Fat Lot of Good. How the Experts Got Food and Diet So Wrong and What You Can Do to Take Back Control of Your Health.* Penguin Random House.

Ede, Georgia Dr. (2024). *Change Your Diet, Change Your Mind: A powerful plan to improve mood, overcome anxiety and protect memory for a lifetime of optimal mental health.* Yellow Kite.

Teicholz, Nina (2014). *The Big Fat Surprise. Why Butter, Meat & Cheese Belong in a Healthy Diet.* Simon & Schuster Paperbacks.

About the Author

Tracey is a holistic health and life coach from Melbourne Australia. She is the founder of The Thriving Place—a global platform to support people to thrive. She is also a wife and a mum of five children.

She has been through some major transformations and healing, from reversing prediabetes at age forty and overcoming a lifetime of emotional eating and drinking habits. By far her biggest healing has come from an autoimmune diagnosis, which saw her break free from co-dependency.

Tracey is also a public speaker, podcaster, and coach mentor.

In 2023 Tracey spoke at TEDx Katoomba and her talk, 'Becoming the Navigator of Your Own Life', can be found on YouTube.

To connect with Tracey, The Thriving Place:
https://www.skool.com/the-thriving-place
Email: tracey@traceymcbeath.com.au
Instagram: @tracey.mcbeath.health